GOD, WHAT THE HECK?!

100 DEVOTIONALS FOR WHEN LIFE SUCKS

By Chantelle Anderson

GOD, WHAT THE HECK?!

100 DEVOTIONALS FOR WHEN LIFE SUCKS

PREFACE

This book isn't meant to be academic. It's more like a training guide, full of quick, insightful lessons that you can use to fight for your faith.

It's the one you pick up when you're thinking about leaving God, as you consider coming back to Him, or when you just need a reminder of why you're determined to stay.

Over the next ten chapters and 100 devotionals, I'll share personal stories to help illustrate spiritual concepts.

Some of them will be from my life B.C. - before Christ - including when I first started my faith journey towards Him. And of course I'll share stories from after He finally saved me on September 17, 2013.

This book will help you believe God when it's hard to, run to Him when you don't want to, and commit to Him when everything is telling you it's not worth it.

To get the most out of it:

- Read each passage of Scripture first - God's words are more important than mine
- Read the devotional that goes with the Scripture
- Read the chapter of the Bible that the passage is in - context is everything
- Journal through the challenges and record your progress
- Use the hashtag #GodWhatTheHeckBook to connect with others doing the same

I hope you will feel loved in the middle of your storm.

In grace and gratitude,

Chantelle

When 2020 started, I was planning to write a book on identity. But instead, I wrote the one I needed to read.

It all began when I got a call from my Mom on Sunday afternoon, February 9th, saying that my Daddy had fallen, and was in the ambulance on the way to the hospital. She wasn't sure if it was serious but said she would keep my sisters and me updated.

By Monday, we got word that the doctors had no idea what was happening but that Daddy wasn't doing well. On Tuesday, my three sisters - Kristin, Amber, and Kristin Marie - and I all headed to the hospital in San Diego.

Walking into Daddy's room for the first time, seeing him - formerly 6'5" and full of life - frail, delirious, and not even able to speak, was almost more than I could handle. I was shocked at how sick he actually was.

There was a glimpse of hope though when, in a moment of clear thought, he realized all of us girls were there to see him and cried happy tears. He couldn't speak but we knew he felt loved.

I fought hard to hold onto that hope and stay faithful he would get better. And he did, for a little while.

After spending five days in the hospital together, we saw Daddy get back to his sarcastic, funny, stubborn self. That was the guy we remembered.

But he was still too weak to go home or be without professional supervision. So over the next two months, he went back and forth from nursing facilities to the hospital for a variety of issues. Each time we were told that the doctors didn't know exactly what was wrong with him but were doing everything they could to figure it out.

Eventually, they diagnosed him with quick onset dementia, but even that seemed like an educated guess.

My sister Kristin and I continued to travel back and forth between LA and San Diego to visit him. Until the COVID-19 pandemic caused all hospitals to shut down visiting hours. Just like that, we couldn't see Daddy at the time he needed us most.

In the middle of all this, I was having a conversation with my friend, Isaiah, and he asked me, "If this chapter of your life had a title, what would it be called?" I immediately responded, "God, what the heck?"

I'll finish Daddy's story a little later. But the whole experience sucked and I was definitely asking God my fair share of questions.

At that point, I was about a quarter of the way through writing this book, and finishing it became my way of staying connected to Earth.

Kristin told me she was thankful for her kids, Kingston and Phoenix aka Missy, because they forced her to keep going. I told her I felt like I could literally quit doing life and be fine. I had nothing that demanded I got out of bed.

I did have family and friends who wouldn't have let me stay in my bed for the rest of life like I wanted to. But in a way, this book became my kid, my baby. It became the thing I had to get up and take care of. Because if I had to feel this horrible I was going to make sure something useful came out of it.

Being all the way honest, I think I'd forgotten how hard life could be and feel sometimes. I'm a naturally optimistic person, was living the life I wanted, and even when it wasn't perfect it was really good.

Which was great but completely unrelatable to people who don't feel like that.

So while this isn't the book I originally wanted to write, after going through 2020, it's the book of survival, questioning, and eventually, restoration that we all need to read.

In that case, I'm thankful to God for putting me in a place to write it, even though there were times I didn't think I'd make it through.

When we find ourselves here, in a place we don't necessarily want to be, a series of thoughts can go through our minds like:

Where am I?
How did I get here?
Why am I here?
When can I leave?

Depending on where we are with God at the time, the language might be a little more colorful or the questions different. But the questioning process is very real.

From there we try our best to answer them. We go to friends, family, social media, "experts," pastors, and anyone else we think might know more about it than us.

In the meantime, we get through it with journaling, meditation, gratitude lists, daily devotionals, and various other kinds of "self-care."

Or, if you're like me, you try to do everything you know you're supposed to. But the end result is bingeing on Law & Order SVU marathons, taking a third nap, another trip to the refrigerator, pouring yourself into your work, or being everything you need to be for everyone else.

Coping is a real thing. We'll talk about that later.

But right now, instead of all that - or maybe in addition to it - we need to go to God. His Word is the only place we'll get real answers.

So here we, are writing and reading this book, doing that. Going to God through Scripture to figure out this whole getting through when life sucks process, together.

Pray for me as I pray for you.

"Your word is a lamp for my feet, a light on my path." - Psalm 119:105

DEAR GOD,

USE EVERY OUNCE OF MY EXPERIENCE
TO HELP SOMEONE ELSE.

AMEN

1. COM

PELLED

(A Conversation About Love)

WAIT.
GIRLFRIEND?
I THOUGHT THAT
WAS ME...

I remember the first time I fell in love. Well, it was high school so who knows if it was real love. But let's go with it because I thought it was at the time.

I walked into my school gym one night for a volleyball workout and there he was, playing basketball on the other court.

He was tall, dark, beautiful, and I had never seen anyone like him before - especially in Vancouver, Washington. He took my number and we talked on the phone almost every night after that for months.

I knew he was "the one." Especially after I met his Mom and she all but welcomed me into the family immediately.

One day I skipped class and rode the city bus across town to surprise him at his school. But I wasn't on campus more than five minutes before a rumor started that I was there to fight his girlfriend.

Wait. Girlfriend? I thought that was me...

Apparently, all the girls at his school - and various other ones - liked tall, dark, and beautiful too. And with all those options, he was not about to be a one-girl man in high school. I left without seeing him.

He called later and the first thing he said was, "Did you come by my school today?"

Turns out you need to be careful when you surprise people, or you might find out a truth you didn't want to know.

After that, we were on and off for the rest of high school. He had other girlfriends, but he always came back to me and I never understood why he didn't just stay there.

Still, even though I hated it, I accepted him back every time.

How often do we go all in - sometimes to the point of losing ourselves - for someone who doesn't love us back? They give us their reasons and excuses, and we listen because we're hoping they'll say something that will allow us to justify staying, again.

It took me a long time to learn that we'll never require love we believe we don't deserve.

That's why we keep going back to people who don't really love us. It's not the kind of love we want, but it's the love we believe we're worthy of.

That's also why it's hard to believe God's love sometimes. In the deepest part of ourselves, we don't believe we deserve to be loved unapologetically or unconditionally.

But we have to. We have to believe God loves us like that because it's the foundation of everything. Literally, everything.

It's true we don't necessarily deserve it. However, God doesn't base His love on what we "deserve." He bases it on who He is. And He gives love because He gives Himself.

God doesn't care that we don't deserve it. He just wants us to accept it, and do our best to return it.

We have to know and really believe that because when we feel loved by God, we'll ride through anything with Him - even these "what the heck" moments.

More importantly, we'll always give Him a chance to explain. We'll listen to His "why." Because we've done it for people who gave us incomplete love. How much more so for the real thing?

So over the next 10 devotionals, we're going to learn more about what it means to be loved by God. Once we understand that, our ears - and more importantly our hearts - will be open to hearing Him about everything else.

Let's study it out.

A STUDY ON LOVE

Please read each Scripture before you read each devotional.
God's words are more important than mine.

THE LOVE BEHIND THE DEATH THE LOVE BEHIND THE DEATH THE LOVE BEHIND THE DEATH THE LOVE BEHIND THE DEATH THE LOVE BEHIND THE DEATH THE LOVE BEHIND THE DEATH THE LOVE BEHIND THE DEATH THE LOVE BEHIND THE DEATH THE LOVE BEHIND THE DEATH THE LOVE BEHIND THE DEATH THE LOVE BEHIND THE DEATH THE LOVE BEHIND THE DEATH THE LOVE BEHIND THE DEATH THE LOVE BEHIND THE LOVE BEHIND THE DEATH THE LOVE BEHIND THE DEATH THE

2 CORINTHIANS 5:14-15

As a reluctant hopeless romantic, this is everything.

What would you pay to save someone you knew was going to disrespect you, stab you in the back, be too ashamed to tell anyone y'all were even cool, and never apologize for any of it?

I don't know if you answered the same as me - maybe you're a nicer person - but my answer, in my best Christian language is, "Not a dang thing!"

After reading some Scriptures and deciding to be more like Jesus, I'd give them forgiveness and maybe a smile or some food.

But it definitely wouldn't be the most important thing to me in the history of things. It for sure wouldn't be my niece or nephew, who I adore. And it absolutely wouldn't be my own life. Yet that's exactly what Jesus did for all of us.

The value of something is determined by what you're willing to pay for it. Jesus paid with His life and God paid with His Son, for us, even if we never choose to acknowledge Him. For us at our best, us at our worst, and everything in between, Jesus gave His life.

Can you imagine that kind of love?

"Jesus died for our sins" has been said so many times in religion that it has lost its impact on many people who say it, including me at times.

But we have to ask ourselves, are we really convinced that Jesus died for us? And are we connected to it?

Not the death, but the love behind the death. The love that motivated the death.

It's the kind of love that was meant to stop you in your tracks, win you over and convince you you're loved, even when you look around and don't feel like it.

This kind of love is to help you remember that you're worth loving, no matter who says you're not. Even when the person saying it is you.

Jesus doesn't want you to be motivated by obligation. He wants you to be motivated by love. To be compelled to live this life with Him and for Him by how much He loves you.

CHALLENGE:

Let this display of love inspire and motivate you to keep fighting for your faith, and for a relationship with God that will carry you through the hardest times.

ROMANS 8:37-39

I used to cut people off immediately.

I was selective about my circle and it was always small. Anyone who made me feel anything I didn't want to feel had to go. Which was a lot of people because healthy boundaries didn't exist.

There were either no boundaries between us or like the Great Wall of China. Sometimes both within the same day.

But when I decided to follow God, I had to work really hard to change that and part of the reason is this Scripture. Cutting people off isn't in God's character so I needed to remove it from mine.

The world tells us that certain people don't deserve our grace or our efforts to forgive. It tells us that it's okay to ghost people without trying to work out issues first, or that we should evaluate people's worthiness before we prioritize helping them.

But thank God He doesn't treat us like that. Even though our behavior hurts Him, He reasons with us, loves us, forgives us, and does anything He can to work it out. He doesn't protect Himself by running.

He never leaves. Never walks away. Never says He'll never speak to us again. We sometimes do those things to Him yet even then, He's there when we change our minds.

If a person acted like that, we might say he was weak and had no self-respect. But God knows who He is. He's just that humble. And loves you that much.

His anger is never bigger than His love.
His hurt is never bigger than His love.
His hatred of your sin is never bigger than His love for you.

You are His weakness, His kryptonite.

He'll let you go because true love includes freedom. But when you're ready to talk, He's ready to listen. When you're ready to come back, He's right there, excited to celebrate.

CHALLENGE:

Meditate on every time you've called on God and He's been there, no matter how many reasons you gave Him not to be.

WE ARE HIS WEAKNESS WE ARE HIS KRYPTONITE

SOMEONE WHO LOVES YOU CHOOSES YOU.

(READ THAT SENTENCE AGAIN)

1 JOHN 4:19

I was crushed.

Have you ever liked someone thinking the feelings were mutual but they weren't?

I remember in high school I liked my best friend at the time. He was beautiful and we were amazing together. Only he said he could never date a girl taller than him. And I wasn't even that much taller than him. Ugh, the struggle.

We've all been rejected in some way before.

Rejection feels like who you were wasn't good enough. Not that what you were doing wasn't good enough. But that you, as a person, were not and won't ever be. Rejection can pierce you straight to the heart if you let it.

I think that's why God made it a point to tell us that we don't have to be afraid of being rejected because He loved us first.

And someone who loves you chooses you. Read that sentence again.

Too many of us have let being rejected by the wrong people make us believe we're not worth being chosen, or that we have to prove we are a million times over.

That's not true.

God, the Creator of the universe, chose you already. He chose you and He keeps choosing you every day.

So the choice for us is not simply to love God. It's always to love God back, enough to choose Him too. And enough to let that be enough.

You were born chosen.

CHALLENGE:

Remind yourself that not being chosen by someone else will never matter as much as the fact that God already chose you.

GOD IS LOVE

PROVERBS 19:22, 1 JOHN 4:7-8

It could all be so simple.

I used to be the queen of absolutely magical relationships until they blow up in your face. Think of Taylor Swift's song, "Blank Space," in a person.

To be fair, the majority of my ex's were really great people, and I'm still on good terms with most of them. But it never ended well.

I spent my entire 20's looking for love, trying to complete myself with imperfect people and incomplete things. I'm still healing from the scars.

Too often we try to define love as gifts, good sex, a "relationship goals" hashtag, money, or loyalty. We'll chase love and try to find it from anyone who looks good, pays attention, or gives off the right "energy."

Those aspects aren't inherently bad and are absolutely ways we can show love. But on their own, none of them are love, or will ever be. God is. When we try to substitute those things for God it may feel like love, but it'll always be the side to the main dish.

God defines love as Himself. We need love, God is love, done, and done. And it really was meant to be that simple. Instead, we go looking for love everywhere else.

Then we get hurt. The imperfect things we go to for unfailing love leave us staring in the mirror with tears running down our faces, pleading with ourselves, "Why is this happening?" That could just be me, but I doubt it.

Objects will always fail under a weight they weren't made to carry. God is the only One who can give and be love for us at the same time.

God gave you a desire that only He could fulfill, on purpose. He wants to be your everything. Let Him.

CHALLENGE:

As you're continuing to build your relationship with God, look for everything
you desire in Him before you go looking for it somewhere else.

1 CORINTHIANS 13:4-8

This is the extended definition of love.

I'm always losing my keys. I usually check my bag first, because that's probably where I left them. Then I check the counter, the bed, the bathroom, my jackets, and wherever else they might be.

But you know what's the most annoying thing ever? When after looking everywhere else, I go back to my bag, dump it all the way out, and there are the infamous keys - right where I already looked - where they've been the entire time.

So annoying. Because if I would've looked hard enough the first time, I would've found them.

It's been the same way with me and God. I grew up going to church and left mainly because I didn't feel or see real love there. I figured God was the problem and went looking for it everywhere else.

It was never sustainable though. So instead of going back to church, I went back to the Book that had been in church the whole time. The Bible. I went back to God.

I realized that when I was attending church the first time I almost never read the Bible. And I for sure didn't study it. Just like my keys, God had been there the whole time, but I wasn't looking hard enough for Him.

"God is love," can be a bit ambiguous without a more practical definition. This passage is like God saying, "I'm love, and love is all these things, so I'm all of these things."

He's detailing how He satisfies each individual aspect of the love we're searching for.

We as people can only try to be an example of God every day. And we fail. But if you're searching for love and haven't looked - I mean like dump out your bag looked - for it in God and His Word, you've been looking in the wrong place.

Whenever you're not feeling or seeing love around you, go back to His Word.

CHALLENGE:

Pick one of the Gospels to read like you're desperate to learn enough about the Author to fall in love with Him.

GOD IS PATIENT.

GOD IS KIND.

GOD DOES NOT ENVY.

GOD DOES NOT BOAST.

GOD IS NOT PROUD.

GOD DOES NOT DISHONOR OTHERS.

GOD IS NOT SELF-SEEKING.

GOD IS NOT EASILY ANGERED.

GOD KEEPS NO RECORD OF WRONGS.

GOD DOES NOT DELIGHT IN EVIL.

GOD REJOICES WITH THE TRUTH.

GOD ALWAYS PROTECTS.

GOD ALWAYS TRUSTS.

GOD ALWAYS HOPES.

GOD ALWAYS PERSEVERES.

GOD NEVER FAILS.

PSALM 139:13-18

Note to self for always.

I'm 6'6". When I started the 8th grade I was 6'0" tall. Then I grew three inches that year, one more that summer, and entered high school as a 6'4", gangly, awkward freshman.

I could also never find clothes that fit me correctly. I wore men's pants that were usually too big in the waist because that was the only way they'd be long enough.

I hated how I looked, wasn't winning any style awards, and the classmates who teased me for it didn't help.

Whenever I would see the popular girls at school, petite, preppy, and looking like they had just stepped out of the classic movie, *Clueless*, I hated myself even more. I used to ask God why He made me like this.

I know I'm not alone. We've all looked in the mirror and said, "God, why am I like this?" That's why I love this Scripture and specifically God's connection to knitting.

The thing about knitting is that it's intentional. If the color or pattern changes it's because you did it on purpose. Especially if you're God and never accidentally skip a stitch.

So when the Bible says God knit us together, it means that every single characteristic we have, God put there on purpose. Everything we hate about ourselves, God loves. Even the things that make us "weak," God put there for a reason.

He knows everything about you because He made everything about you. You can be completely real with Him. No hiding. Nothing has to be scripted or pretty. You're allowed to be the hot mess you feel like sometimes and God still won't agree with your negative self-talk.

He still thinks you're wonderful because He's God and He makes masterpieces.

One of my favorite parts of this passage, though, is that He'll never forget us. I can worry about being forgotten sometimes but here, God says that we can't even count the thoughts He has about each of us.

So just remember, in all of your imperfections, you're wonderfully unforgettable to God.

CHALLENGE:

Stop questioning how God made you and find ways to celebrate it instead.

EVERYTHING YOU HATE ABOUT YOURSELF, GOD PUT THERE ON PURPOSE.

ALL
IN.

MATTHEW 22:36-39

Confession: I want to get married one day.

I don't know if or when it's going to happen, but I hope it does. So let's say I was getting married and when it was time to say the vows, it went like this:

"Chantelle, do you take [insert dude's name] to be your lawfully wedded husband?"

"I do!"

"[Dude], do you take Chantelle to be your lawfully wedded wife?"

"I do...most of the time...like 80%...but yeah..."

Yo. I'd be outta there so quick! And keeping it real, you know you would too. Neither of us would put up with that because we know when it comes to being in a relationship, real love includes full commitment.

Even before God, when I was in a non-exclusive relationship in the name of "freedom," I remember feeling my heart drop and stomach turn at the thought of the person I was with being with someone else. I couldn't deny that I wanted to be the only one.

So if we, as imperfect humans, can expect someone to be committed to us, how much more so should the Creator of the universe expect it? How much more so does He deserve it?

God doesn't want to be in a one-sided relationship any more than we do. And He won't. God knows who He is, and He knows His worth. So while He does love us with everything He has, He asks for our all in return.

The best part is that God's "all" is way more than ours. It's like we give Him $100 and He gives us $1 million back. We definitely get the sweet end of the deal here.

God is a hopeless romantic and exclusivity is what makes your love story with Him "happily ever after."

CHALLENGE:

How can you give God more of your heart, soul, and mind? What have you been holding back from Him? Give it to Him.

JOHN 1:35-39

You don't have to love Jesus right now.

In my first year in Turkey playing basketball, I met this guy on social media. At first, I didn't know much about him other than that I liked his pictures and he was living in Atlanta.

It turned out he played ball and even though he was cool, I didn't trust an athlete who was that fine - sorry to any athletes reading this. Thankfully though, we had about four months to talk before I came back to the States.

As I got to know him, he turned out to be thoughtful, funny, and a one-woman man on principle. I eventually fell for who he was.

I was playing in Atlanta for that WNBA season so once I got back, we were basically inseparable for the rest of the summer.

I would eventually learn that building a relationship with God is kind of the same process.

When the men in this passage asked Jesus about where He was staying, Jesus told them to come and see. He didn't say, "love me," "obey me," "give up your life," or anything else. Instead, He invited them to hang out with Him.

Jesus knew if they hung out with him, they'd get to know Him, and would eventually love Him.

Jesus doesn't expect us to automatically fall in love with Him at first sight. We don't need a cartoon moment like cupid shooting us with an arrow or a miraculous experience.

At first, there may be things that grab our emotions. But a true, lasting relationship with God comes from getting to know the character of who He is.

Then we'll fall in love to stay in love.

Think of it like dating Jesus. Like dating anyone else, you don't have to know right away if you're ready for "'til death do us part." Just make time for Him, talk and listen regularly, and build your relationship on purpose.

If you love Jesus already, that's amazing. Keep dating Him, because we all want healthy marriages.

But if you don't, that's okay too. He's completely fine with you coming to see. You just have to decide He's interesting enough to get to know better.

CHALLENGE:

Seek Him, to find Him, to know Him, to love Him.

COME AND SEE.

YOUR VALIDATION COMES FROM YOUR MOST IMPORTANT RELATIONSHIP.

MATTHEW 3:16-17

The goal is to please God.

"She has no idea!" I complained to my spiritual mentor.

The day before, I had taken a flight at five in the morning from an out of state speaking trip so I could make it to a day of back-to-back ministry meetings that didn't end until one the next morning. When I woke up after finally getting some sleep, I felt like I'd been hit by a truck.

I had a meeting scheduled that morning with a friend to look at some Scriptures but asked if we could move it to the next day. She was great with it. When I called to notify the other woman who was going to join us, she told me I should not have rescheduled, implying that I wasn't doing enough for God.

As I got off the phone I felt defeated and wanted to stop trying. I prayed and called my spiritual mentor.

There have been many times I've felt like people expected me to be perfect, and that no matter how much I did or how hard I worked, I'd never be good enough. In times like those, I go to this Scripture.

What I love is that at the beginning of Jesus' ministry, before He preached, healed, or saved anyone, God said He was well pleased with Him. All Jesus had to do to please God was make a decision to obey Him, and walk His path. It wasn't about the ministry numbers to God. It was about the heart to follow.

Your validation comes from your most important relationship. So when you let people's words or actions consistently make you feel unworthy and defeated, you're valuing those relationships too high.

There are times that you'll be doing your absolute best and it still won't be good enough for some people. But God is "well pleased" when you decide to follow Him step by step, no matter what you accomplish or what other people think about it. Now that's love.

He's the only One you need to worry about pleasing.

CHALLENGE:

Give more power to God's opinion than you do to people's, even your own.

PSALM 136:1-26

Are you taking applications for the love of your life?

The other day I was talking to someone who didn't really know me, and I felt like they were doubting me a little too much.

There was literally a point in the conversation where I wanted to slide them my resume like, "I'm sorry, you must not know who you're talking to, so let me let you know so we can have a real conversation."

Have you ever thought that? It can't just be me, right?

I feel like that's what God does in this Psalm. It's Him sliding His resume of love across the table to us.

Anytime we doubt God we can use this resume to prove His track record of love that started long before we were born.

And for God, the love language He speaks is action. He doesn't expect us to take His word for it without backing it up. He acts, and just in case we didn't recognize it as love, He reminds us that love is why He did it.

Then there's the concept of forever.

God's love never ends. It never runs out. No matter what happens, how hard life is, what you've said, or what you've done. No matter how much time has passed. It never ends and it never runs out.

But what do we use a resume for? The purpose of a resume is to convince the person making a decision that we're qualified for the position we're applying for.

So think about this. God, the Creator of the universe, the most powerful Being in the history of everything, is applying to be the love of your life, forever. Like, what?!

Seriously. The power is in your hands on where this relationship goes. He's asking you to be in it for better or for worse because He's fit for the job. That love you're searching for is what He has been giving you and will continue giving you, if you're down.

Once you decide to trust God's love for you, then everything else - literally everything - can be viewed in the context of that love.

So are you in? Will you trust the God of forever behind the resume?

Write God's resume of love in your life and keep it somewhere
that will remind you of who He is when you doubt.

GOD'S LOVE ENDURES FOREVER.

GOD'S PATIENCE ENDURES FOREVER.

GOD'S KINDNESS ENDURES FOREVER.

GOD'S GOODWILL ENDURES FOREVER.

GOD'S MODESTY ENDURES FOREVER.

GOD'S HUMILITY ENDURES FOREVER.

GOD'S HONOR ENDURES FOREVER.

GOD'S CONSIDERATION ENDURES FOREVER.

GOD'S GRACE ENDURES FOREVER.

GOD'S FORGIVENESS ENDURES FOREVER.

GOD'S GOODNESS ENDURES FOREVER.

GOD'S TRUTH ENDURES FOREVER.

GOD'S PROTECTION ENDURES FOREVER.

GOD'S TRUST ENDURES FOREVER.

GOD'S HOPE ENDURES FOREVER.

GOD'S PERSEVERANCE ENDURES FOREVER.

GOD'S RELIABILITY ENDURES FOREVER.

GOD'S LOVE ENDURES FOREVER.

2. GOD

'S PLAN

(A Conversation About Timing)

THIS COULD NOT BE REAL LIFE.
BUT IT WAS.

On April 18, 2020, from 9:02 PM to 10:04 PM, everything changed. Ironically enough, that day was actually the best I'd felt since Daddy first got sick.

Before I got the call, my roommates and I had just finished a living room dance party. Then I got on a Facebook messenger call with friends and we were laughing hysterically as we changed the filters on our faces, taking screenshots of how funny we all looked.

There was even a point where I thought, "Oh wow, this is so fun. I actually feel normal."

Then at 9:02 PM, my phone rang and I saw it was Mom. I immediately knew something was wrong because Mom doesn't call late. So I got up and started walking to my room to take the call. As soon as she spoke I could tell she'd been crying.

She said, "Hi Chantelle. Daddy's blood pressure is 50 over 20. His body is shutting down and they don't expect him to make it through the night."

I collapsed to my knees on the stairs.

She continued, "If he passes away and they call me in the middle of the night, do you want me to call you?"

"Yes, please," I whispered.

"Okay, I will. I'm going to call Amber now."

"Okay thanks, Mom. Love you."

I couldn't move. What was happening? No, not tonight. Not ever but for sure not so soon. Daddy was supposed to get better. This story was supposed to end with happily ever after. What was going on?

Three minutes later Kristin called me and suggested we call Daddy on three-way as we had done several times while he'd been in the hospital. Daddy couldn't talk but his nurse, Agnes, was going to hold the phone up to his ear so we could talk to him.

We told him we loved him more times than I can remember. We told him that he was the best Daddy ever and that everything we are was because of him. We told him funny stories that we remembered and how thankful we were for him.

We finished talking to him at 9:42 PM and at 10:04 PM I got the call from Mom that his heart had stopped.

I don't remember much after that. All of a sudden I looked up, it was 11:47 PM, and I was still sitting at my desk with my head in my hands trying to make sense of what just happened.

This could not be real life. But it was.

Why do people we love die?
Why do kids get cancer? Or anyone for that matter?
Why are there incurable diseases?
Why are innocent people murdered for their skin color?
Why do we have desires that God says no to?
Why are some people born into poverty and others into wealth?

If God is good, powerful, and loving, how is all of this His plan?

This chapter could easily be the inspiration for the title of this book. Knowing God is all-powerful while at the same time looking at the state of the world like, "God, what the heck?!"

It's easy to trust God's plan when what's happening is what we think should happen. "Yeah God, great plan!"

But when God's plan hurts, and what's going on is completely the opposite of anything we'd ever choose, we have questions...

Does God really love me?
Is the Bible really true?
Is God actually good?
Does He really have power?
What's the point of all this anyway?

I know in the last month alone I've asked myself all of these questions and then some. And that's okay.

It's like any other relationship with someone you love. You can disagree, question, cry, and maybe even yell. But it's not over until one person decides to leave and never come back. It's still a relationship until one of you decides it isn't worth fighting for anymore and quits.

That person will never be God. He will never walk out because the fight is always worth it to Him.

Although there are many exhausting things we go through, I think situations we don't understand are the hardest not to quit on. At least, that's the truth for me.

So in this chapter, we're going to talk about believing in God's plan anyway.

During our conversation I'll go deeper into some of my difficult experiences as illustrations. I never want to paint this life as all roses without acknowledging the rain that allowed them to grow. But I'll label those devotionals on the first line with a trauma or sensitive subject warning.

The one thing I want you to walk away with is a decision not to quit on God no matter what. Stay right here and fight for your relationship with Him, because He's fighting for you.

Let's study it out.

DEAR GOD,

ALLOW ME TO SEE HOW YOUR PLANS

ARE BETTER THAN MINE.

AMEN

A STUDY ON GOD'S PLAN

Please read each Scripture before you read each devotional.
God's words are more important than mine.

THIS ISN'T HEAVEN

REVELATION 12:7-12

This is about to get deep.

I'm an idealist. I believe in justice, doing the right thing, and good intentions. My default is to give people the benefit of the doubt until they show me why I shouldn't. And even then I still want to give them another chance.

For someone with that mindset, this world is exhausting.

On the day I wrote this, I saw a video of a man in handcuffs who suffocated to death as a cop knelt on his neck. I was sick to my stomach because that was the fourth situation I'd read about like that in the previous two weeks. Injustice towards people who look like me makes me physically feel the brokenness of this world.

Every time it happens, I have to remind myself that Earth isn't Heaven.

For some reason, we act like this is supposed to be a great place. We act surprised when horrific, disgusting things happen. But the truth is, we were born right into the middle of the most brutal spiritual war ever.

And just like a physical war, if you're in the middle of a battlefield walking around like you're on a playground, you're definitely dead.

Living in a fallen world doesn't allow us to limit the degree of evil we see or face. We don't have that liberty or control.

And so how do we look at this from a spiritual point of view?

By acknowledging the fact that this world is full of people who are broken by sin, including ourselves. When appalling things happen, that doesn't necessarily mean they were part of God's plan. Some tragedies are the results of war.

So when you find yourself questioning God in the face of injustice, pain, or suffering, remember this isn't Heaven, and it's not supposed to be. Satan lives here. He's mad and trying to make things as bad as possible so you doubt God and go with him for eternity instead.

Don't make his job easier by expecting this world to be something it's never going to be.

CHALLENGE:

Frame things spiritually. Feel your feelings but keep them from running away with you by reminding yourself of the spiritual war around us.

JOB 38:1-11

We don't get to make the rules.

Growing up, I used to ask Daddy a million questions. He frequently said that "why" was my favorite word.

Usually, he would take the time to explain things to me so I could learn and understand. But there were other times when, instead of explaining, he would say, "nunya."

"Nunya" meant, "none of ya business." It was kind of his way of saying, "because I said so." I used to get so mad - especially as someone who wants to understand everything - because at that point I knew I wasn't getting an explanation.

God's the same way. There are some things for Him that fall under the category of, "nunya," or, "because I said so."

Just like we had to obey our parents because it was their house, their rules, this is God's world, God's way. We didn't create the universe or anything else in it.

So when we ask God our questions that are begging for answers, He might take the time to explain all the details. He also might say "nunya."

It can be tempting to feel frustrated when we don't get the answer. Yet that's why we talked about trusting God's love.

The goal is to trust God's love so much that we look at everything in that context. If we do, even when He says "nunya," we won't be afraid. Because when you're confident someone loves you, you don't doubt their motives or intentions. You trust.

If everything is in the context of love, it gives us perspective on some of God's actions that we might be tempted to question:

Giving us the Bible with the directions we need for life is loving.

Blessing us with great outcomes when we follow the Bible is loving.

Giving us the freedom not to follow is loving.

Using the painful consequences of our choices to turn us towards Him is loving.

Turning a hard situation into the best possible outcome is loving.

And honoring our final choice not to choose Him is loving.

Everything God does is loving. Let go of your need to understand everything and trust that in some way, God's love is behind it.

Continue building your faith to the point where you look for the love in every situation, even the hard ones.

GOD IS ALLOWED TO SAY, "NUNYA."

DEUTERONOMY 30:15-20

"God, are you really in control or not?"

One thing I struggled to understand for a long time was the intersection between God's sovereignty and our free will.

God's sovereignty means He has the ability and the right to do whatever He wants. But then I thought, "If God is in control and He's supposedly good, why do bad things happen?"

The answer, many times, is free will. Terrible things happen because we also have choices, and sometimes we choose wrong.

God has the ability to control us and everyone else. He won't though, because taking away our free will wouldn't be loving. To violate us in that way is the farthest thing from who God is.

Instead, He gave every single person freedom of choice to love Him, but with it came the freedom to ruin things.

It's like a card game with God as the dealer.

He dealt us a hand, and because this is a fallen world, some of the cards suck. Then He gave us a Book to teach us how to play, with directions for every situation, so we can make all the right moves.

God totally set us up to win.

But there's one rule: He can't cheat. He can't play our hand for us - because of the whole love equals freedom thing.

So He tries His hardest to prove Himself to us, to convince us we should listen. And then when we make a play, whether we listened to Him or not, He works to adjust our lives for the best possible outcome. God is that powerful. Sometimes we just make the wrong play.

Like in Spades when your partner bids Nil and she's trying to make sure you win all the books, but then you lead with a three of hearts. She's going to look at you like, "What the heck are you doing?"

Sometimes I'm looking at God asking, "Why is my heart broken? How is this a good plan?" And He's looking right back at me saying that this is the best possible plan, taking into account my decision to make moves He didn't cosign.

This life isn't an example of what God's plan looks like, or it'd look like Heaven. Instead, it's an example of what it looks like when we play our hand the way we want instead of the way God said.

This is why, in His love, He's begging all of us to choose His way in every moment.

Validate your ability to choose God's way or not. Recognize that God doesn't agree with other people's choice not to choose Him, especially when it hurts you.

YOU HAVE FREE WILL

GENESIS 45:4-9, 50:19-20

This can be a sensitive topic.

My path before following God had extreme highs and lows, without much in between. I've survived abuse, rape, and suicidal thoughts. I've struggled with self-harm, eating disorders, and depression.

All while living a very public life. The whole time I was trying to smile and "fix" myself with everyone watching. It felt a lot like trying to change my shirt in a car, parked in a crowded parking lot, in broad daylight without flashing the people staring at me. Not easy.

When I said I wanted to be great at basketball, I didn't understand how heavy the weight was that came with living in the spotlight. I struggled to carry it for a long time.

But now, not a day goes by that I don't thank God for who it made me into. I see how it could have broken me. Instead, it taught me the lessons I needed. And it built the character to sustain the responsibility of God's calling I didn't know existed.

When I sit in Bible studies with women now, I'm grateful for even my hardest experiences because I can meet them in their pain and relate.

Even before the international movement, the words "me too" were powerful. They build a bridge of compassion and understanding between our separate experiences so we can support each other. I know now that was God's plan for me all along.

We see that with Joseph as well. There were so many people who wronged him in awful ways. He was sold into slavery, accused of attempted rape, thrown in jail, and forgotten for years.

God didn't agree with what those people did to him. They went directly against God's desire. Yet God was able to take care of Joseph every step of the way. God didn't prevent him from being thrown in jail when he was falsely accused, but He did bless him while he was there. God can bless you anywhere.

God used everything that happened to Joseph to both teach and elevate him. The teaching came from the trials, but the elevation came as Joseph remained faithful and obedient to God through them.

In the end, Joseph ended up where God wanted him to be, despite the thorny path in getting there. And in His mercy, God used him to save his family, even though you'll see as you read the rest of the story that they were part of the reason his path was so hard.

No one else can stop God's plan for you. But you can stop it by choosing not to follow Him because of what the path looks like.

Know that God can use anything for good, despite people's actions. Look for God's plan, even in the worst situations.

YOUR PATH

BUILDS THE CHARACTER

NEEDED TO SUSTAIN

THE WEIGHT

OF YOUR CALLING.

ROMANS 4:18-21

Character is the key.

My parents got a divorce when I was in 3rd grade. Mommy moved back to Southern California, taking my two sisters, Kristin and Amber, and me with her. Daddy stayed up in Vancouver, Washington to continue working as a perfusionist.

During the year, we talked to Daddy on the phone often and he faithfully paid child support. Then every summer we'd live in Washington with him, his new wife who we called "Mom" instead of "Mommy", and her daughter, Kristin Marie.

One time in the spring, Daddy was in San Diego for a work conference and drove three hours to see us for 45 minutes, just to go right back. That was all the time he had off of work and he refused to be that close without seeing us.

I can't remember ever questioning something Daddy said he was going to do. Not even once, because he proved himself so many times.

When Abraham looked at God, he saw that certainty. Even when he was faced with a situation that was by all indications absolutely hopeless, Abraham still believed in what God promised him. He didn't doubt it.

Abraham wasn't delusional or numbed out. He still acknowledged the facts of the situation. But he didn't let the facts discourage his faith in the faithfulness of God. He didn't let his physical reality distract him from God's spiritual capability.

Abraham's unwavering belief allowed him to live his life as if what God said to him was true, even in a "hopeless" situation.

The one constant in a forever changing world is the unchanging character of God.

I'm so thankful I had Daddy who was an example of that for me before I knew God. It has made it easier to see God's character.

I do realize others have different experiences. Close friends have shared with me that when their physical fathers were absent or unloving, it was hard for them to view God as a loving Father who's always there.

It's true that our relationships with our human fathers can be complicated. But projecting that onto our spiritual Father will handicap us.

When God tells us who He is, we have to work really hard to believe Him. Because the biggest part of trusting a plan is trusting the person who has the plan. And the biggest part of trusting a promise is trusting the person who made the promise.

So what do you believe about the character of God? Trust that He is who He says He is so you can also trust His plans.

Take the things God says about Himself at face value, and look for the ways He proves them true.

BELIEVE WHAT GOD SAYS ABOUT HIMSELF

EXODUS 13:17-18

God, did we miss a turn back there?

The single life can be hard sometimes. Especially because before I chose to follow Jesus, even when I was technically single, I was single but occupied.

Once my life changed, a lot of my previous relationship behavior had to go. I was impure, immoral, manipulative, disrespectful, hateful towards men, and the list could go on.

I fully believe that if I would've gotten married before finding Jesus, and maybe even shortly after, I'd definitely be divorced by now. Maybe even in jail. Just saying.

I see why God would've had to transform my character in advance to prevent me from ruining my future marriage. On the other hand, I feel like a kid in the back seat on a road trip like, "Dad, are we there yet?"

Some days I can relate to the Israelites as they followed God out of Egypt.

They knew they weren't going far away - the trip that took them 40 years should've only taken about 11 days. What they didn't know was that they would have to conquer 31 different Kings once they got to the Promised Land.

After over 400 years of slavery, they weren't mentally or spiritually ready for those wars. So God protected them from it.

While they were questioning God's route, His timing, and even His faithfulness for taking them on a journey that looked pointless, He was developing them into the people who could win the battles they needed to win, to posses what He already had for them.

God will keep you in the desert as long as it takes to get you ready for the Promised Land. He sees the entire journey, where you are, where you're going, and gives you a plan that accounts for all the things you don't see.

Marriage isn't a promise but in hoping for it, there have been guys I was really asking God for, and I was mad when He said no. Then when I saw who they truly were, I was like, "Wow, God, you were really looking out on that one." He's protected me so many times from the things I wanted.

God does promise a joyful, purposeful, and impactful life as we follow Him. But if it feels like He's taking you the long way, trust it. To Him, it's more important to protect and prepare you than it is to give you His promises on your timing.

There's always love behind the delay.

Pray and ask God to help you trust His path more than your vision.

YOU AND YOUR DESTINATION ARE BEING PREPARED

A LIGHT ON MY PATH A LIGHT ON MY PATH A LIGHT
ON MY PATH A LIGHT ON MY PATH A LIGHT ON MY
PATH A LIGHT ON MY PATH A LIGHT ON MY PATH A
LIGHT ON MY PATH A LIGHT ON MY PATH A LIGHT
ON MY PATH A LIGHT ON MY PATH A LIGHT ON MY
PATH A LIGHT ON MY PATH A LIGHT ON MY PATH A
LIGHT ON MY PATH A LIGHT ON MY PATH A LIGHT
ON MY PATH A LIGHT ON MY PATH A LIGHT ON MY
PATH A LIGHT ON MY PATH A LIGHT ON MY PATH A
LIGHT ON MY PATH A LIGHT ON MY PATH A LIGHT
ON MY PATH A LIGHT ON MY PATH A LIGHT ON MY
PATH A LIGHT ON MY PATH A LIGHT ON MY PATH

PSALM 119:105

I'm just trying to get where I'm going.

When I was in middle school, my family used to go camping every summer. We had a family reunion where everyone would bring their tents and campers for four days of potlucks, clamming, campfires, and sleeping under the stars. I always looked forward to it.

The only thing that was annoying was when I had to get up and go to the bathroom in the middle of the night.

I'd have to rummage around the tent to find the flashlight someone kicked in their sleep. Then unzip the tent door and walk to the bathroom in the big house, which was about a football field's distance away.

The walk was scary sometimes. Even with a flashlight, it's just enough to light your path and help you find your way, but not enough to light the world around it so you forget you're walking in the dark.

When God compares His Word to a light on our path, that's what I think of. Then I remember how many times I was desperately trying to find my way through life but my Bible was closed. It was like I left the tent without my flashlight and ended up lost.

For us, trying to live life without the Bible doesn't make sense if we're trying to find God's plan. Prayer is important because that's when we pour our hearts out to God - we'll talk a lot about that in this book. But reading His Word is how He talks back and gives us the direction we're asking for. It's the lamp for our feet.

Sometimes life will feel like jumping over obstacles on the way to the bathroom, and you'll need to hold onto His Word even tighter. And although it's not going to light the whole world or make you forget about the darkness around you, it will be your personal light on your own path.

As long as you keep using it, you'll be able to see each step ahead of you and keep walking towards the plan God has for you.

CHALLENGE:

Don't try to walk through this life without God's "flashlight." Make reading the Bible part of your daily routine. Tip: If you don't know where to start, try the Gospel of John. It communicates Jesus' heart.

NOT MY WILL BUT YOUR WILL BE DONE. AMEN.

MATTHEW 26:36-39

It's okay God. I'm still here.

I really believed, like really truly did, that God was going to heal Daddy. And He didn't. That doesn't mean I did anything wrong or didn't have enough faith. It just means that whatever happened was God's time.

This can be a hard thing to accept. But sometimes God doesn't rescue us from whatever it is that we're begging and trusting Him to.

Case and point: Jesus prayed three different times for God to take away the call for Him to die on the cross. He begged God through tears and bloody sweat to change His mind about it. And God said no.

We have to be okay with God not always answering our requests with the answers we're asking for. We have to be willing to pray, "Not my will but your will be done," and then not hate God when His will turns out to be different than ours. That's where submission comes in.

Allow the emotions and go to your own Garden of Gethsemane, even when you don't want to. Take your inner circle of people with you, and get vulnerably open about how you feel. Then pray until you're able to follow God's plan wholeheartedly.

If the Son of God had to fight in prayer for three hours, we shouldn't expect the fight to be easier for us.

For me, this looks like going into my prayer closet and having an honest conversation with God about how I'm feeling. Most of the time that's me telling Him, usually in tears, that I don't like the plan in front of me. But even as I'm honest with Him in the moment, I also don't leave until I'm ready to face what's next.

In this situation with Daddy, what was next was not what I wanted. Sometimes, God says no to what we're asking Him for. But we have to trust Him enough to realize that saying no doesn't mean, "I don't love you."

Only then will you have the strength to pray for His will above your own.

CHALLENGE:

What "yes" are you praying for that you would be upset at God for answering "no" to? Ask Him to help you surrender your will to His. And remember, He always loves you.

GOD

IS BIGGER

ECCLESIASTES 8:16–17

It's all relative.

My six-year-old nephew, Kingston, is my favorite little boy ever. He's smart, artistic, athletic, and I swear he's going to be a star. He's also not immune to regular kid meltdowns. Sometimes my sister, Kristin, will make a decision he doesn't agree with and all of the sudden in his mind the entire world is falling apart.

He definitely lets her know how he feels, usually in a very animated way.

Then Kristin will look at him, with love and amusement, and remind him, "Bud, you are six. I'm your mom and I love you. I'm going to take care of you."

Because at six there's no way he can understand jobs, bills, ministry, raising a family, and everything else she and her husband, Josiah, are managing. In her love though, she's considered him in all of it.

When I read this passage of Scripture, I can't help but wonder how many times a day we put God in Kristin's position. How many times do we question things that we couldn't possibly understand?

It's incredible when I think about the fact that every detail of your life is as important to you as my details are to me. And God knows and cares about them all at the same time.

There He is, courting, managing, leading, and loving each person through each situation. At the same time He's making sure we have every chance to choose Him and get to Heaven. Not only for us right now but for every person who's ever lived.

That's overwhelming. There's no way we could comprehend even a fraction of what He's doing.

Our thoughts, feelings, and ideas feel so significant. And they're definitely valid to God, just like Kingston's are to Kristin. But when you look at the bigger picture, they're a small part of everything that's going on as a whole.

When you remember that God knows things you don't know and sees things you don't see, it will be easier to trust His plan and find peace on the ride.

CHALLENGE:

Picture God responding to you as Kristin does to Kingston: "You're still young compared to eternity, I'm God, I love you, and I'm going to take care of you."

This Scripture is a hard truth to accept sometimes.

I hate that Daddy died. Whenever I think about not seeing his smile again or looking at his kind eyes, I cry. Whenever I think about all the questions I want to ask him but can't, or things he wanted me to do that I didn't listen to, I cry harder. I hate feeling like this.

When it happened, everyone around me lovingly told me to take a week off, with no responsibilities. Yet even after that week stretched into ten days, I wasn't prepared to return to the routine of my life. My feelings weren't done being unstable.

Thankfully, the pandemic and the stay-at-home orders had already scaled back my life without me having to set boundaries, explain myself to people or contend with the pressure that I should be doing more.

I know the severity of this pandemic has been disastrous for so many people. However for me, mentally and emotionally, the required distancing during my grief process has been an unanticipated blessing.

The energy it took to put on a nice shirt and walk to my desk for a Zoom call was significantly less than getting all dressed up to drive across LA and pitch a new client.

It was easier to hide my tears on Zoom when someone inadvertently said something that triggered me. It happened almost every meeting for at least the first couple of months.

I could turn off my camera and dry my tears instead of trying to sneak out to the bathroom with my head down, hoping no one noticed.

Nothing is more unpredictable than pain. So having the flexibility to move in and out of my emotional breakdowns while still participating in everyone else's "normal" was one thing I was consistently grateful for.

This Scripture is a promise of good in every situation - like a silver lining in every storm. The concept is easy to accept when the through-line between what happened and what good could possibly come from it is obvious.

But for the tragic, heartbreaking experiences that are hard for us to understand, this concept takes more faith to accept.

It doesn't mean that all situations are good. They're

not. It does mean that good comes from all situations. Those are two completely different things.

This promise of good in every circumstance gives us the hope to get out of bed and keep going through the rest of life, even in the worst times.

I don't know what hard situation you're struggling to see the good in or what the silver lining will turn out to be. It may take you some time to find it. But it will be there.

God doesn't promise a life without rain. He just promises that no matter how dark the cloud and how much the water threatens to drown you, for those who love Him there will always be a silver lining behind it.

CHALLENGE:

In the times that you don't agree with God's plan, look for the silver lining. It's always there.

GOD WORKS IN ALL THINGS

3. TRA

INING

(A Conversation About Trials)

WHY WAS THIS SO HARD? WASN'T
BASKETBALL SUPPOSED TO BE FUN?

Freshman year at Vanderbilt, before I'd ever played a game or even went through a practice, Coach Foster and I stood in the gym looking up at the rafters at the retired jerseys. Wendy Scholtens - Vanderbilt's all-time leading scorer - was the only women's jersey hanging there.

In a moment of boldness, I told Coach that I wanted to break her record. When I said it I had no idea what it would take and I'm sure he knew that. But he didn't laugh or discourage me. Instead, he replied, "Okay. If you're willing to work for it, I'll help you."

Fast forward to one day during pre-season conditioning, we ran so many stairs that I physically couldn't stop my legs from shaking. I was laughing through tears at the craziness of it as I teetered, step by shaky step, back to the locker room.

That entire first summer I was useless in any pick-up game that followed a conditioning workout. I ran around aimlessly trying to keep up after losing the power to control my muscles. When the season started, I cried at least three times every week during practice. Literally.

My goal of owning the scoring record seemed like a fantasy and at that point, I felt lied to. Why was this so hard? Wasn't basketball supposed to be fun?

I asked my position coach, Coach Gaudet, about it and I'll never forget his answer.

He said, "You know, the game isn't always fun. There are times when you're tired and feel like you can't breathe. You're getting elbowed and beat up. But what's fun is after the game, when you're in the shower winding down, and you're like, 'Man, we just kicked their butts.' That's when it's fun."

That was a lesson for basketball and life. The training part almost always sucks. What's fun is the results of the training. When you can do something today that you couldn't do yesterday.

In basketball, it was when the same girl who could barely get through workouts and cried all the time in practice ended up becoming Vanderbilt's all-time leading scorer, and getting drafted 2nd overall in the WNBA. There's another women's jersey in the rafters.

In life, it's when someone you would've cussed out a couple of years ago disrespects you, and now you can smile and love them anyway. It's when your ex tries to come back for the 10th time and you're strong enough to say, "Nah," and keep it moving. It's when you lose your job and instead of freaking out, you automatically respond in faith because of all the times God has come through for you.

That's when you look back and are thankful for the training.

Legendary basketball coach, John Wooden, said, "Sports don't build character; they reveal it."

I would say sports do both. They show you where you are in your character and then help you grow from there. All trials do that. Sports just subject you to trials in a structured environment that trains you for real life, whereas other trials happen in real life.

God uses struggle in our lives in a way that usually doesn't feel good. But it does help us in the long run. So as we study this together, think of anything you've trained for or worked to be excellent at. That's your parallel when I talk about basketball.

Because the truth is, you probably understand most of what God is doing in principle. You just have to relate it to your life.

Then you have to trust Him like you would trust a great coach, trainer, or teacher who loves you and is working to make you better.

Let's study it out.

A STUDY ON TRAINING

Please read each Scripture before you read each devotional.
God's words are more important than mine.

MARK 4:35-41

Wait, God. You want me to move again?

When I first became a Christian, I was living in Houston, working a corporate sales job and building my speaking business on the side. After almost four years and encouragement from a mentor, Brad, I decided to go into full-time entrepreneurship as a corporate trainer and speaker.

Two months later, my church asked me to go on a mission team to help plant a new church in Miami. That meant I would have to pick up everything, including my infant business, and move to a more expensive city.

When I prayed about it, I really believed God wanted me to go. So I went, working to scale my business as I lived off of the money I had saved.

Six months later as I was getting business traction in Miami, I got asked to move again. This time it was to Los Angeles to help build the Arts, Media, and Sports Ministry. Given my background, going made complete sense. My prayers this time were a little different though.

"God, You know I need to make money right? You want me to move across the country to one of the most expensive cities in the world when my business isn't even self-sustaining yet? Bible studies aren't going to pay my bills You know. Like, You can't be serious..."

Obviously, I wasn't super faithful.

This is why I can totally relate to the disciples when they questioned Jesus in the middle of the storm. Their fear of what they were going through made them doubt God's love and protection.

The goal is to get to Jesus' level where not even the scariest situations panic us because our faith in God is that strong.

When they woke Him up, He immediately calmed the storm right before their eyes. It reminds me of one of my favorite quotes by Leslie Gould: "Sometimes God calms the storm, and sometimes God lets the storm rage and calms His child."

I did end up moving to LA on faith, with no idea how long it would take my business to be able to support me.

Within the first month, I signed my largest business client to an 8-month contract. That made sure my business would be self-sustaining for the entire year. Two months later, after speaking at a conference that I only attended because I was in California, I signed a speaking contract with Google that paid me my largest, single-engagement speaking fee to date.

God came all the way through. He always does.

When you feel unsafe, forgotten, or not considered in the middle of your storm, remind yourself that God is powerful enough to handle whatever you're going through. It's frightening to ride out the waves sometimes, but He gave you Jesus for those exact moments.

CHALLENGE:

Run to Jesus for help instead of trying to handle your problems on your own. He's the only one with the power to calm the storms.

EVEN THE WIND AND THE WAVES OBEY HIM

ROMANS 5:3-5

Winners are made through suffering.

I used to get my butt kicked every day in practice by this guy named Don. He was 6'6", and one of the ROTC cadets who regularly practiced against my team to help get us ready for games.

I was used to physically overpowering the smaller girls I played against, and that didn't work with him. At all. I needed to be more fundamentally sound. Coach would tell me to run a play and I physically couldn't do it because Don was right there, stopping me.

Those first practices felt like suffering for real. Sometimes I'd stand on the court, tired and in pain, looking around like, "Who signed up for this?" It made me question if I really wanted to be the best or if just being talented was enough.

Gradually, as I got better, I stopped getting outplayed and even started to challenge him a little. Soon, every day was a battle for both of us. As I held my own, either of us could win on any day in any drill.

When practicing at that higher level against him became the norm, I could compete with anyone.

It became the character of who I was as a player.

In learning to do life God's way, the process is similar. He teaches us from His Word, the playbook, and then causes or allows real-life situations that challenge us to apply what we've been taught.

That usually feels like suffering, and we'll probably default back to what we've been doing all along. That's who we are. We haven't built up our spiritual character yet. And at times we'll even question if it's worth it.

As we continue to persevere through the trials and repeatedly work to respond God's way, His teaching changes from what we know to who we are. Through perseverance in suffering, knowledge becomes character.

Just like I started to make the right basketball plays even against Don, godly character means you make the godly choice, even in the hardest situations.

Then you'll be able to walk in hope because when you play the right way, you always put yourself in a position to win, now and in eternity.

When you're going through a hard time, look at it as a drill to make you better. Get competitive and focus on playing God's way.

SUFFERING
PERSEVERANCE
CHARACTER
HOPE

JEREMIAH 12:5

Get ready to run.

The summer after my sophomore year in college, I made the USA Basketball team for my age group. We ended up going to Beijing and winning a gold medal in the World University Games.

Afterward, USA Basketball flew us to Hawaii for an exhibition game against the Women's Olympic Team. I was ecstatic to play against my idol, Lisa Leslie, and the other women I'd had posters of since high school.

I figured they would be better than us because they were professionals. But I definitely thought, being considered the best college players in the world, that we'd at least compete.

I was wrong. I don't remember what the actual score was but they beat us by something obscene like 80 points. There was literally nothing we could do to stop them. They were just that good.

Overall, the trip left me inspired to see the level I would hopefully get to soon. I knew I wasn't ready to run with them yet. But I would be.

That's something we don't always like to hear but is still true.

Sometimes, we're just not ready.

God can give us a vision that is ahead of our character. He wants to take us there, but we haven't become the people who can compete at that level yet. So instead of throwing us into something we can't handle only to watch us get destroyed, God prepares us where we are.

He isn't trying to be cruel when you go through adversity or even get rejected. He has a plan for you to "run with horses."

Life is about progression and our current challenges are preparation for greater ones to come. He's getting you in shape first.

As God makes you into the person who can do what He's prepared you for, you have a choice. You can either beat yourself up for not being ready and question God as to why it hasn't happened yet. Or, you can focus on getting better wherever God is currently training you.

Then trust that in His time, He'll put you in a position to be who He's trained you to be, to make the kind of impact you were created to make.

Don't put pressure on yourself, or on God, to make anything happen right away. Patiently and humbly be flexible with the process of leveling up.

YOU'RE BECOMING.

GOD DIDN'T AGREE BUT HE'LL HELP YOU FIX IT

PROVERBS 19:3

Note to self: Father knows best.

One day in elementary school, Daddy told me to go outside and get the mail. My church shoes - the shiny, patent leather slip-ons - were right by the door so I put them on and started out.

Daddy said, "Go get your other shoes because those ones are slippery and you're going to fall." But I, being lazy, told him I'd be ok and went anyway without changing my shoes. I got halfway down the driveway and what do you think happened?

Exactly what Daddy said was going to. I fell, cut my knee open, and started crying. There was blood running all the way down my leg.

Sometimes our situation has nothing to do with God's actions and everything to do with ours.

It would have made zero sense for me to get mad at Daddy for asking me to get the mail when I was the one who didn't listen to him about putting on different shoes.

It's the same thing when we choose to disobey God and end up in pain or difficulty because of it.

God isn't happy that we're hurting but it was our disobedience that put us there. And just like my Daddy, He warned us beforehand in His Word that doing it our way would hurt.

We have to be careful in those instances to take responsibility for our actions instead of blaming God for the consequences.

Still, when I came back bleeding and crying, you know what Daddy did? He hugged me, dried my tears, and helped me clean it all up. Because he loved me and that's what good Daddy's do.

God is a good Daddy too. The best. He's not going to hold a grudge when you get hurt doing something you weren't supposed to. He wants you to run to Him so that He can comfort you and help fix the situation from there.

To do that, you might have to choose not to be angry at God for the fact that you got hurt, or let go of your shame for disobeying in the first place.

CHALLENGE:

Is there anything you've been blaming God for? Instead, run to God's Word and ask Him how to clean up the mess from wherever you are.

WORK OUT YOUR OWN SALVATION
WORK OUT YOUR OWN SALVATION
WORK OUT YOUR OWN SALVATION
WORK OUT YOUR OWN SALVATION
WORK OUT YOUR OWN SALVATION
WORK OUT YOUR OWN SALVATION
WORK OUT YOUR OWN SALVATION
WORK OUT YOUR OWN SALVATION
WORK OUT YOUR OWN SALVATION
WORK OUT YOUR OWN SALVATION
WORK OUT YOUR OWN SALVATION
WORK OUT YOUR OWN SALVATION

PHILIPPIANS 2:12-13

God, it's me and You.

I think one constant in the life of many Black Americans is figuring out how to successfully be both Black and American at the same time. When I became a Christian, I added one more identity that seemed to fight with the other two.

This year, it felt like the world discovered the battle I go through, and not everyone was willing to listen with a heart to understand. I was in many conversations about race and sadly, the ones with self-identifying white Christians were more difficult than those with white people who weren't Christian.

After one such conversation, I found myself on the floor, shaking and crying from anger. I couldn't believe I'd been spoken to that way. I wanted to cuss, scream, blast him on social media and cut off everyone who I thought agreed with him.

It was at that moment I thought of this Scripture and had to make a decision. There's a reason the Bible says, "Work out your salvation with fear and trembling."

I usually read the NIV version but I actually like the King James Translation better with this verse because it adds the word, "own." "Work out your own salvation with fear and trembling."

Sometimes, it will be excruciatingly hard to do the righteous thing. You'll want to cut someone off, sweep something under the rug, or just numb out. Pushing through will take work, tears, and conviction.

But no one else is responsible for your relationship with God. It's your own salvation.

So in each moment, do whatever it takes to stay faithful to God. That includes recognizing that other people are also working out their own salvation, independent of you.

Making it through this life can be traumatizing, whether you're with God or not. It's better with Him though. Stay, no matter what it takes.

CHALLENGE:

Don't let other people get in between you and your relationship with God. Work it out with Him, in His Word, always.

ISAIAH 42:3-4

Rehab is part of training.

Before my fifth year in the WNBA, I tore my Achilles tendon. I'll tell you the whole story later, but I was devastated.

It was demoralizing going from being able to do almost anything to not even being able to move my foot on its own. Some days, I came into rehab motivated and ready to work. There were a lot of other days though when I could barely overcome my sadness to get up and get there.

One of the only bright spots during rehab was Kara, my physical therapist. I used to tell her she was my angel. Her smiling face and beautiful spirit always made me feel better.

Kara was gentle, but she wasn't weak and never let me off easy. Pushing my body, in its broken state, towards healing was painful and tedious. Sometimes it felt like I was being pushed too far, but Kara always knew when to stop.

Little by little, she worked me back to health. The best part was that she believed I could come back and helped me trust that everything was actually going to be okay. And it was. I was back on the court that same year.

When reading this prophecy about Jesus, it's encouraging because He's like our spiritual physical therapist.

When we're hurting, feeling broken, weak, or on the verge of being suffocated by life, He'll do whatever it takes to gently and lovingly nurse us back to health.

He always believes in your comeback so He won't just leave you where you are. But He's not reckless or inconsiderate.

Jesus knows that in order for you to grow, He must heal you first.

It may be uncomfortable, and difficult, but you're never broken beyond Jesus' ability to comfort and repair.

CHALLENGE:

Memorize this Scripture so when you're going through anything that feels like too much, you can remind yourself that Jesus is gentle with you in your struggles.

JESUS WON'T LET YOU BREAK

DEAR GOD, SHOW ME MY TEACHERS. AMEN

ISAIAH 30:19-22

God ruined my life to get my attention.

Tearing my Achilles tendon wasn't my first injury, but it was the one that finally redirected me to God. Before that, I had injury after injury, break-up after break-up, and several other unexpected incidences. I felt like I couldn't catch a break.

Once I tore my Achilles I was finally like, "Ok, what the heck?" I realized my way wasn't working and that I obviously wasn't in control. For the first time in years, I was open to seeing what God had to say.

As I learned more about Him, I could look back at my life and see how many times He had been trying to get my attention. Just like in this passage, "my teachers" were hidden. I couldn't see them because I wasn't looking.

Pain forces us to open our eyes.

It's ironic that 2020, in a lot of our minds, was going to be the year of vision. And it was, in a bigger sense than we realized. In a historic way, God removed many things from our vision that were blocking us from seeing Him. Not what we necessarily wanted, but what we needed.

I always say that some people need a tap on the shoulder and others of us need a 2-by-4 upside the head. I'm the latter.

Trials are meant to turn us back to God in any way we may have turned away from Him. The best part is, we don't have to find our way alone. God will give us step-by-step instructions to direct us as we go.

In times when it feels like all you're eating and drinking is adversity and affliction, instead of saying, "God, why is this happening?" ask Him, "What are You trying to show me through this?"

Then ask yourself, "Have I thrown away my idols? Has God been first in my life?"

If the answer is no, then God is trying to use what you're going through to get your attention. He's calling you closer to Him through something that He knows will open your eyes.

Have you been missing your teachers?

CHALLENGE:

Pray. Ask God to show you your teachers and the lessons
He wants you to learn.

ARM YOURSELF WITH:

TRUTH

RIGHTEOUSNESS

THE GOSPEL

FAITH

SALVATION

THE WORD

EPHESIANS 6:10-17

It's never about people.

My relationship with Daddy wasn't perfect. We were two prideful, opinionated people who didn't always see things the same way and got into it quite a few times over the years.

There was one time in particular that stands out to me. I don't even remember what we fought about, but I do remember it ended with me leaving and us both saying we'd never speak again.

I called my sister Kristin, told her what happened, and in the most gentle way possible she changed my entire thought process with a few Scriptures, including this one. She reminded me that it was Satan who wanted me and Daddy not to be close. That was his plan.

I called Daddy to apologize. He said he forgave me. But when I asked to visit for Father's Day coming up he said no. I was so hurt, but I didn't stop trying.

Instead, I drove from LA to San Diego to drop off his gift from Nike on the porch. On my way back, I called him and told him to look outside. When he got it, he asked me to turn around and come hang out for a little while. I did, of course.

One of the hardest things for me to learn was to blame the sin on Satan and not the person. I had to realize I wasn't fighting Daddy.

This Scripture will save relationships if you follow it. Because there will be times when you look at someone and dealing with their behavior is the last thing you want to do. Even with people you love.

But we have to realize that at the root of everything - literally everything - is a spiritual battle against Satan and his army. No matter what it is, what it looks like, or what it feels like. It's not about people, even when people are involved.

That doesn't mean we subject ourselves to unnecessary abuse. It just means acknowledging the fact that as we're working out our salvation with fear and trembling, Satan is the one trying to steal it from us.

In the next chapter, we'll see Jesus put this into action. But for now, know that your battle isn't against people and that God has given you everything you need to fight it.

Don't start a single day without arming yourself for the spiritual battle ahead.

CHALLENGE:

Take your eyes off people and choose to see the spiritual war behind their actions. Only then will you know how to fight.

I CORINTHIANS 15:57-58

Sometimes you have to take the hit.

One time my friend Jessica and I were at the beach, doing one of my favorite things ever, jumping waves.

Normally, I go out until the water is a little below my waist and then every time a wave comes, I try to jump high enough so it doesn't knock me over. The goal is to stay above the biggest part of the wave so I can ride it out instead of getting hit by it.

Then Jessica showed me this other game she liked to play. We still went out to the same depth, and we chose which foot to plant on the ground. That was the foot we couldn't move.

When a wave came, instead of jumping, we met it head-on. The goal was to stand there without letting the wave knock us over or make us move our feet.

It was so fun! I definitely got knocked over a few times. But every time I was excited to get back up and face the next wave.

In the middle of the game, I looked at her and said, "Wow this is just like that Scripture about letting nothing move you!"

That game is life. Things happen every day that come and threaten to knock us down, to uproot where our feet are planted.

We're going to fall sometimes because we weren't expecting the situation, or it was just that big. Or, because we're so used to "jumping" them using our talent, money, or access that we haven't built the mental, emotional, or spiritual muscles to withstand the hit.

But our victory comes from keeping our hearts and minds planted on Jesus. It comes from getting up and viewing each wave as another chance to get stronger. Because the end goal is not an easy life but an eternal one.

Anything that doesn't kill you makes you more useful to God. And if it does kill you, then as long as you're walking with Jesus on Earth you'll be living with Him in Heaven.

Jesus promises to never give you more than He'll help you with. He promises to be there. He promises to bless your wholehearted effort. And ultimately, He promises that His team wins in the end, even when it looks like a loss in the middle.

Stand firm on these promises and let nothing move you from them.

Adopt the mantra, "let nothing move you." Use it to help you stand firm on the promises of God when something threatens to knock you down.

LET NOTHING MOVE YOU

1 PETER 1:6-9

Prove it or build it.

Losing Daddy shook my faith in a way I hadn't experienced before. I had to ask myself, "Do you really believe what you believe? Do you believe God is who you say He is?

I was at a crossroads. If God was who I said, then I needed to continue believing His promises even though my heart was broken. I had to turn to Him at my lowest point and act like He would be there. I had to have the faith I preached about.

Or, I could change my picture of God into someone I agreed with instead of who He is. I could give in to my pain and the fact that I didn't want to believe the hard truths in the Bible. Or I could start ignoring Him all together and go back to living the life I had before.

I can't remember a time since becoming a Christian that choosing God was so conflicting. But when I did choose Him, He was there.

You don't know who's real until you go through the toughest times and see who leaves and who stays. For me, God was the One who was always present, never had something else to do, and knew to show up without me asking. It was like, "Wow God, you're really loyal!"

I learned two things about my faith:

One, that it was strong enough to survive an experience that challenged me to my core and come out praising God on the other side.

And two, that my trust in God to meet my emotional needs wasn't as strong as I thought it was. Because when He did, I was surprised by it.

That's why God tells us to rejoice in hard times. They give us the opportunity to prove that our faith is genuine, or help us see the places where it may not be as genuine as we thought.

Whichever way, the result will be praise, glory, and honor. We either have the faith to survive the trial or an on-the-spot chance to build it on the way to our end goal of salvation.

With that though, there will always be a crossroads. You will always find yourself with a decision to make. In the middle of your trial as your faith is being proven genuine and purified by fire, will you turn towards God in trust or away from Him in doubt?

Let your trials prove your faith genuine or help you build genuine faith.

Thank God for giving you the chance to see where your faith really is and grow where needed. As you go through trials, turn toward Him always.

BUILD YOUR

FAITH

4. S

AFE

(A Conversation About Protection)

THEN I WENT TO FIND JOHNNY AND FOUGHT HIM FOR HITTING MY SISTER.

Kristin was so excited about her gift for Mommy.

We were riding the bus home from school one day - I was in 4th grade and she was in 3rd - and she couldn't stop talking about the plant she was bringing home for her.

We got to our stop and I got off the bus first. Then Johnny, a boy we didn't like at all, jumped off the bus and took off running towards our apartment complex.

Kristin got off the bus without her plant, crying and holding her eye.

Through tears, she explained that Johnny had called her plant ugly so she called him ugly. In return, he slapped her, making her drop her plant that broke as it hit the floor.

I was furious.

Right away, I borrowed a neighbor's wagon to put Kristin in and pulled her all the way home. I grabbed a bag of frozen veggies from the freezer and put them on her face. Maybe all a little over-dramatic, but that was our relationship. I didn't play about protecting my little sister.

Then I went to find Johnny and fought him on the neighborhood playground for hitting her in the first place.

When we think of God's protection, a lot of times we think of Him preventing things from happening to us. And there are times for sure that He moves us out of harm's way.

In many situations though, that would require Him stepping on the freedom of someone else, which we already talked about God won't do. He loves us all too much to force His way on any of us.

For that reason, God's protection often looks like causing or allowing someone to experience the repercussions of messing with His kid instead of preventing the situation altogether. He'll fight for us but that doesn't mean we won't get hit.

It's important that we know this because it takes an incredible amount of trust to run to God crying and ask Him to intervene instead of blaming Him for whatever made us cry in the first place.

In the book of Psalms, we see David navigate this process often. He starts out questioning God, crying, and even complaining sometimes. Yet he finishes by praising God and asking Him to pay his enemies back for the wrong they did to him.

One thing that's difficult about waiting for God to fight for us is that life taught many of us to fight for ourselves. Life also taught us that when we can't fight for ourselves, we end up with wounds that require extensive time to heal. That's not something I readily volunteer for.

Once you learn to defend yourself at all costs, waiting for someone else to do it - especially when it doesn't happen right away - makes zero sense to you. Even when that someone is God. Story of my life!

So how do we stop fighting every battle ourselves and trust in God's protection? I'm learning that more and more every day so in this chapter, we can do it together.

Let's study it out.

A STUDY ON SAFETY

Please read each Scripture before you read each devotional.
God's words are more important than mine.

1 PETER 5:8-9

Don't fall for it.

The other night as I walked around my neighborhood talking on the phone, I noticed a guy walking in the street, parallel to where I was walking on the sidewalk. He wasn't super close, but he was close enough for me to notice, and walking at the same speed I was.

I looked ahead of me and saw another man on the sidewalk standing about the same distance away. They didn't look any different than anyone else I had seen in my neighborhood, and up until then I'd always felt safe.

That time though, as I saw the men flash each other a look, something felt off. I stopped walking and the man in the street stopped too, acting nonchalant but suspicious for sure. I hesitated. Part of me was afraid that if I turned around, they would think I was judgemental for supposing they might be dangerous.

Then I remembered a podcast episode I had done where we talked about how too many women prioritize not hurting people's feelings over their own safety. I had been that woman before and didn't want a repeat. So I turned around and started walking quickly in the other direction, glancing over my shoulder to see if they were following. They weren't.

When I got back to my house, I applauded myself for paying attention and being brave. It's true that I didn't know if they were dangerous or not. Still, better to be alert and safe than caught off guard and sorry.

Spiritually, this is how we need to walk through life. We're in the middle of a spiritual war, remember? We might not be sure of people's intentions but we definitely know Satan's. He's on Earth, not happy about spending eternity in Hell, and working to take as many of us with him as possible.

He'll try to make us so comfortable that we think we don't need God or cause so much pain that we doubt God's love and walk away from Him. He's patient enough to sit and watch or wear you down little by little.

Satan is not your friend. You don't just annoy him. He hates you. Always has, always will. And he will do whatever it takes to convince you to turn away from God and follow him.

That's why the Bible says to be sober-minded. Go through life aware that there are two powers of this world: one who loves you and the other who hates you. Only then will you be able to resist him, letting nothing move you, and locking arms with others who are doing the same.

If we're going to talk about protection, you need to know who God is protecting you from. And the answer is Satan. God is protecting you from being lured into Satan's trap, both in each moment and for eternity.

CHALLENGE:

Don't let Satan catch you off guard with weak faith. Treat life as the spiritual war it is by keeping your armor on and your sword sharp.

SATAN HATES YOU

JOB 1:6-12

Pain and protection are not mutually exclusive.

It was about 9:30 at night. I was watching TV and doing research for a project when I got an innocent text message from someone asking for advice.

When I read it though, I immediately felt sad, hurt, and guilty about Daddy's death. My mood changed and though I really wanted to help that person, I couldn't do it right then.

The next day I was talking to God about this dilemma. How the heck was I supposed to go through this life as someone He's called to help people, and also as someone who was so easily reduced to a puddle of feelings?

How was I supposed to survive? How was I supposed to safely and effectively be me? How was this Him protecting me?

It was one of those driving in the car, bawling your eyes out as you question God, prayers. And when I'd gotten all my questions out and paused just to cry, a thought that felt powerful and kind at the same time popped in my head, and absolutely blew my mind.

"Protection isn't the absence of pain, it's the absence of danger."

I was like, "Wait, what?"

As I pondered that insight, I realized that even though the pain I felt in any triggering situation led me to also feel unsafe, it was true that with God, I wasn't in danger. Continuing to help people would leave me vulnerable, yet wouldn't put me in harm's way any more than it had before.

From then on, when I've been in situations that feel hurtful, I repeat the words in my mind, "I'm safe. I'm safe. I'm safe." It reminds me not to let my discomfort distract me from the reality of God's protection.

When we're feeling pain, we can assume we're in danger, like we're going to be harmed. But with God they're not always the same thing.

Job is the best example of being safe in the midst of pain.

God was literally bragging about Job. When Satan responded with accusations and wanted to test him, God allowed it but set limits by forbidding Satan to take his health. Then later as the testing continued, God removed the limit on Job's health but still forbade Satan to take his life.

Job didn't know it but his life was safe. God protected

him, even as he was hurting immensely.

Our life may not always be this intense, but we can be sure that God is protecting us from things we don't even see.

Something else that may be hard to accept is that even if God did take our lives, as long as we're saved, we're on our way to Heaven. And in the end, that's the safest place to be.

Being in God's hands is always safe.

It can feel like God isn't protecting you when you're hurting. But in those moments, remember what His Word says, go back to the Scriptures about His character, and believe that He will love you through it.

Whether the pain is part of God's plan or a casualty of life, God will protect you.

CHALLENGE:

Remind yourself that you're safe, even when you're hurting. Then go to God and tell Him how you feel, even if it's not pretty.

PROTECTION IS NOT THE ABSENCE OF PAIN, IT'S THE ABSENCE OF DANGER.

GENESIS 3:1-7, 13-19

Thank God I didn't get everything I wanted.

My parents were super strict growing up. I wasn't allowed to listen to most of the popular music, my shorts had to be longer than my fingertips when I put my arms at my sides, and I wasn't allowed to date.

I was always breaking the rules though. I listened to my friends' music at their houses, changed into my cut-off shorts in the bathroom at school, and started sneaking out my bedroom window to chill with guys. It got to the point where I was doing whatever I wanted behind my parent's back.

And it was so fun. Until it wasn't. It turned out I had horrible judgment and that what I wanted to do was totally different than what was actually good for me. But my parents already knew that and listening to them would've prevented my most embarrassing and traumatizing experiences.

We also see this dynamic at the beginning of creation when Eve first and then Adam chose not to listen to God.

The story is infamous. God commanded them not to eat the fruit because it had consequences they wouldn't understand. Satan came, told them something different, and instead of standing firm on what God said Eve believed He was holding back from her. They chose to disobey and look at where that got us.

Too often we think that by setting boundaries God is trying to take away our fun and make our lives miserable. Really, He's trying to protect us because our limited understanding makes it hard for us to judge what's harmful.

As much as many of us don't want to admit it, we know it's true. Think back to everything you wanted to work out but didn't, and now you're like, "Phew, dodged a bullet on that one!" I bet it's more often than not.

As your Father, God tries to protect you from a lot of dangerous situations by preventing them altogether. There are some negative incidents that are going to happen regardless of our efforts, but many other pitfalls can be avoided.

When you trust God's love and character, you'll see His restrictions as protection, even when it feels like He's holding out on you. That perspective will make it that much easier to obey.

We have two choices. We either cross the line and find out why it was there, or trust that the One who put it there had a reason rooted in love.

When you don't like God's boundary, assume it's to protect you because He loves you.

PREVENTION IS PROTECTION

TAKE THE WAY OUT

I CORINTHIANS 10:12-13

Jesus be some self-control in these single streets!

The other night I wanted to text a guy I shouldn't be texting and say things I shouldn't be saying. My feelings were cheering, "Go for it!" and my mind was sitting there like, "Chantelle, don't you dare." It felt exactly like in the cartoons when they have an angel on one shoulder and a devil on the other. The struggle.

So I picked up my phone, got out of bed, and walked down the hall to my roommate Lee's room. I said, "Hey, can you hold this for me tonight and give it back to me in the morning please?" She said, "Yep!" and did exactly that.

Side note, that's the benefit of having friends on the same path. She didn't even have to ask why. She already knew, and there were other times she'd asked me to do the same thing.

Oh, the single life. I always tell single women that Satan knows "your type" and he will not hesitate to send them. He's so petty.

Temptations are constant for all of us, no matter how strong we are. That's a guarantee. Sometimes it can feel like no one understands, and you may have different triggers or desires than someone else. But the ways we're tempted and the feelings that come with them are common. We're all going through similar things.

Because of that, God is like, "Ok, I got y'all." In His faithfulness, He'll never allow a temptation that's too strong for us to get out of, even when it feels impossible. He'll protect us from being forced to sin.

Sometimes the way out is to run. Sometimes it's to speak up. Sometimes it's remembering the last time it didn't turn out how you wanted so that you stop yourself from walking into that situation again. Sometimes it's to call someone you know is going to help you do what God wants.

Prayer at that moment for strength is always part of the strategy and you can combine it with any of the other options.

When you're facing temptation, you can beat it with God. You don't have to give in to the voice or the feelings telling you to do it. And taking God's way out will always protect you from the consequences that would come from rejecting it.

CHALLENGE:

Get in the habit of praying when you're tempted and then look to God's Word for a way out.

PLAY YOUR GAME   DON'T GUARD YOURSELF
PLAY YOUR GAME   DON'T GUARD YOURSELF
PLAY YOUR GAME   DON'T GUARD YOURSELF
PLAY YOUR GAME   DON'T GUARD YOURSELF
PLAY YOUR GAME   DON'T GUARD YOURSELF
PLAY YOUR GAME   DON'T GUARD YOURSELF
PLAY YOUR GAME   DON'T GUARD YOURSELF
PLAY YOUR GAME   DON'T GUARD YOURSELF
PLAY YOUR GAME   DON'T GUARD YOURSELF
PLAY YOUR GAME   DON'T GUARD YOURSELF
PLAY YOUR GAME   DON'T GUARD YOURSELF
PLAY YOUR GAME   DON'T GUARD YOURSELF

JAMES 1:13-15, PROVERBS 6:27

Let your coach do his job.

When I was playing basketball in college, teams would often try to get me in foul trouble so I'd have to sit on the bench. As long as I wasn't on the court they didn't have to worry about how to stop me from scoring. To do that, they started putting in their second-string players to foul me so I would react.

I fell into their traps over and over and over again. I'd get hit... hit back... get a foul... yell at the refs... make the refs mad... get called for more fouls... sit on the bench and make it harder for my team to win. It was a vicious cycle.

Coach Foster once told me, "Chantelle, you guard yourself far more often than anyone else guards you." He'd add, "Focus on playing your game and let me handle the refs." Then he would yell at them for me.

I understood what he was saying. It just felt impossible to change my default reaction from one of anger and lashing out to letting someone else handle it.

Still, I kept working at it, and once I learned how to do my part and let Coach do his, I stopped fouling out so much and we won more games.

In this situation, God is like a coach. He's not the one sending temptations. He's the one trying to calm us down and fight our battles. Except God can't protect us if we're giving into any desire that threatens to make us do something reckless. It's only a matter of time before we "foul out," no matter what God does.

It's hard to change what we're used to doing and the desires we're used to giving in to. But the desire to please God and "stay in the game" has to be stronger than the ones to be right, loved, wanted, or powerful. Then we'll be able to respond differently when we're tempted.

God isn't sending things to tempt you any more than Coach was telling them to hit me. He's trying to give you every opportunity to win at life, protecting you in the process.

But you also have to quit guarding yourself.

CHALLENGE:

Don't blame God for what tempts you. Instead, focus on making
the right choices and let Him focus on protecting you.

YOU'LL NEVER WIN A SPIRITUAL

BATTLE WITH EARTHLY WEAPONS

LUKE 4:1-13

This escalated quickly.

One time I was waiting after school for my basketball game to start and a classmate said something disrespectful about Kristin, who was - of course - my sister and best friend. I told her to take it back and she didn't. So we fought and I ended up throwing her down a flight of stairs.

No one said anything because if I got caught I wouldn't be able to play in the game that night. So she just cried and learned never to say anything about Kristin again.

Before I became a Christian, that's how I fought my battles. It was either a physical fight, a cuss out, or a cut-off. Usually the last two. If it was a personal battle, I coped by numbing or doing something impulsive.

But once I learned that everything is a spiritual battle, I had to learn different ways of fighting.

In this passage, we see Satan tempting Jesus in the wilderness. He attacked Jesus' identity in God, offered Him food when He was hungry and used Scripture out of context.

Every single time, Jesus fought back with Scripture. He didn't try to reason with Satan or outsmart him. Jesus picked up His spiritual sword and used it against Satan's advances.

Listen to me on this one: Satan is trained.

He will use the same tactics against us that He used against Jesus. He's been doing it since Adam and Eve and knows Scripture better than any of us.

This is not a fight we can opt-out of. When we win one battle, he'll look for a better time to come back and try again.

Winning with your own power, intellect, strength, or scrappiness isn't an option either. Satan will not be overpowered. Those traits can help, but using them alone without Scripture is spiritual suicide.

God gave you spiritual weapons because earthly weapons will never win spiritual battles. Your protection will come from your sword.

Use it like Jesus did.

CHALLENGE:

Start memorizing one Scripture a week to protect yourself in times of spiritual attacks.

EVERYONE

WILL ANSWER

TO GOD

HEBREWS 10:30-31

"When they go low, we go high."

When Michelle Obama first used what would eventually become one of her most famous catchphrases at the 2016 Democratic National Convention, many of us responded with a collective, "Yaaasssss!" We loved her for acknowledging the public slights and insults we received daily, while also calling us higher.

Going high when they go low sounds inspiring, but in the moment, it's tough!

For me, it's the hardest when I feel intentionally disrespected. I know God calls me to be the bigger person but sometimes, I want to use their behavior to justify my retaliation. Maybe you can relate.

In those cases, this Scripture can be both our comfort and our warning.

It's a comfort knowing that no act of revenge on our part will rival anything God already has waiting for them if they continue to disobey. They're going to have to answer to Him, especially when they come after one of His children.

And it's a warning because I don't want to fall into the hands of God either! He's going to hold me to the same standard He holds them to, and that temporary feeling of vengeance isn't worth His punishment. Not at all.

It can be tempting to take things into our own hands. But this is the assurance that when we let God deal with it, it will get dealt with in a way He deems fit. Some people call it karma, but really it's us and everyone else living with the results of our obedience or disobedience to God.

Those consequences might be in private because, at the end of the day, people have to go home with and as themselves. Or they might be in public because what's done in the dark comes to the light eventually.

Either way, do everything in your power to be the bigger person and trust that God's got the rest.

CHALLENGE:

Let it be enough that people who hurt you will fall into the hands of God. Make sure you're not falling with them.

1 PETER 2:19-23

God, I trust You.

Nothing makes me want to argue more than when someone lies about me.

I take who I am and my reputation seriously. If I do something questionable and someone says something about it, okay. But when someone lies and it makes me look like someone I'm not, I feel like that's an issue that needs to be corrected.

There was a time when someone at work twisted my words, misrepresented my beliefs, and accused me of things I didn't do. I was livid.

Initially, since it happened on the internet, my first thought was to call her out on social media. I wanted to make a video detailing exactly what was said and why I was right. I had all the evidence and Scriptures ready to show she was lying and prove my innocence.

At the end of the day, I chose not to. I said what I needed to say to those in charge but stayed quiet oherwise.

Even though it felt like I was punking out and letting her get away with something she should have to pay for, I chose to move forward without proving anything to anyone. Part of the reason was this Scripture.

If anyone could've proven Himself right, it was Jesus. He was perfect. He could have easily argued His defense or just killed anyone who was doing Him wrong. He didn't though. He showed us what it looked like to be the bigger person in literally a life or death situation.

He knew that because God is fair, in the end He would get what He deserved and the people crucifying Him would have to contend with God. So Jesus entrusted Himself to God. He showed us the ultimate display of trust in God's protection by confidently putting His entire self, present and future, in God's hands.

It's a deep form of self-denial not to fight back. That doesn't mean we're not honest about who we are, what we need, and what we have or have not done. Jesus repeatedly communicated that.

At a heart level, however, you have to trust that God will protect you and judge justly in whatever happens between you and others. Imitate Jesus by putting your entire self under whatever God chooses to do.

When you do, you can be confident that He will judge justly.

Be wise and honest about yourself. But when it comes to fighting to prove yourself to people, trust God to do that for you.

ENTRUST YOURSELF TO GOD
ENTRUST YOURSELF TO GOD
ENTRUST YOURSELF TO GOD
ENTRUST YOURSELF TO GOD
ENTRUST YOURSELF TO GOD
ENTRUST YOURSELF TO GOD
ENTRUST YOURSELF TO GOD

"MINE."
– GOD

ISAIAH 43:1-2

Confession: I don't play about the person I'm in a relationship with.

I love when people post social media pictures of their significant other with the caption, "Mine."

Funny enough, the other day I was on Instagram and saw this artist post about how his wife was replying from his account to all the women sliding in his DM's. She sent her picture, questioning why they were in her husband's inbox in the first place when according to his profile he was very clearly married. One of her messages literally said, "What you doin' here?"

When I saw that, I laughed out loud and thought, "That's definitely something I would do."

I'm an, "I wish a chick would," type of woman - in my best Christian language, with the claps included. Some might say that's crazy or possessive but whatever.

On the other hand, I'll also do anything for whoever is mine. In my opinion, being possessive is only dangerous when it's abusive. Otherwise, it's just providing and expecting exclusivity.

So when I first read this passage, the word that jumped out to me was "mine." God is letting us know that He's possessive of us. We are His. He also summoned us by name, meaning we're not randomly His. He was specific and intentional about us being His.

And because of that, He's serious about protecting us.

It's guaranteed that we will go through trials in our lives. The type will vary. But even though waters, rivers, and fires - literally and spiritually - may threaten us, God promises He'll be right there.

So when you feel overwhelmed by sorrow or obligations, consumed with anger or hate, or going through an attack from the enemy that threatens to take you captive, know that none of it will be too much for you.

God is always going to defend what's His.

CHALLENGE:

Protection comes with possession. Don't leave God during hard times. Stay and trust Him instead.

JOHN 6:65-69

There's nowhere else to go.

One time in high school, Daddy and I got into this really nasty fight. I don't remember what it was about but both of us did a lot of yelling and by the end of it I was sobbing in anger.

I stormed downstairs to my room, packed a bag, and called my friend to come get me. In true high school fashion, I was leaving and never coming back home.

I ended up staying with my friend Ty. She attended the college right near my high school so it was the perfect arrangement. For two weeks we had a blast. I loved not having to get permission from anyone to do whatever I wanted.

Then one day, Kristin and I stayed after school and ended up talking about the whole situation. Through our conversation, I realized that even though I was having fun, I missed the safety of home. It's not like Ty's place was unsafe. But it wasn't home, especially without Daddy there to make me feel safe.

Kristin told me to call Daddy. And even though I didn't want to because I was still mad, I did miss him and want to go home.

As soon as he picked up the phone and I heard him say hello, I started bawling. He cried too and I drove home right after that.

When I read this passage, I feel like the disciples totally get me.

Jesus had just preached an extremely controversial lesson that honestly sounded crazy. Instead of having faith and asking for more understanding, most of the crowd decided to leave.

Then Jesus turned to His twelve Apostles, His best friends, asking them, "Do you guys want to leave too?" Peter - this is the part I love - basically replies saying, "Naw, there's nowhere else to go."

It's interesting that Peter didn't say he didn't want to leave. He just states the fact that there's nowhere else to go because Jesus is the way to eternal life with God.

Listen. Some days, we're going to respond exactly like Peter. Something is going to happen in life and what Jesus says about it is going to make us want to leave. We're not going to agree or like how it made us feel.

But if we believe Jesus is the way to eternal life

with God, then there's nowhere else to go. It's impossible to be safe when our salvation isn't secure.

So you can disagree with Jesus and then realize you don't want to be spiritually homeless and stay. Or you can leave and aimlessly look for safety outside of the protection, love, and care of your Father.

CHALLENGE:

Resolve to stay. No matter what happens, promise to stay with God, for better or worse. Because home with your Father is safe.

YOU'RE ONLY SAFE WITH THE ONE WHO CAN SAVE YOU.

5. OPEN

WOUNDS

(A Conversation About Grief)

IT'S OK TO BE SAD.

Grief - keen mental suffering or distress over affliction or loss; sharp sorrow; painful regret. [1]

I was lying on my bed, mindlessly scrolling through Instagram, then Facebook, then Instagram again. I knew I shouldn't be numbing out, but I was. "It's okay to be sad," I told myself. That permission felt good, and necessary, though I wondered why.

I continued into my thoughts...

When did it stop being okay to cry? Was it the first time we did it in front of someone who made fun of us for it? Or when someone spanked us and told us not to cry? Was it when someone took advantage of the vulnerability shown through our tears? Why do we work to stop ourselves from crying even when circumstance insists on it?

As I was having that inner conversation with myself, a separate thought - softer yet more powerful - appeared. "Don't waste the pain." That voice was right. The pain needed to be put to use.

So I got up and walked to my writing desk where I sat and wrote this to you. I wanted to go back to feeling numb. But I figured that if I sat in these feelings with you, we could get through them together, with God.

I'm not going to tell you I'm sorry for your loss or that I hope you feel better. It's true, but I know that doesn't help you in any way other than to show my good intentions.

I do want to tell you that it's okay to grieve. Because if you read and relate to this chapter, you're not thinking about something minor like the last time you stubbed your toe or cut your finger.

No, if you end up really feeling this chapter - maybe it was even the first one you turned to - it's because you have either been through or are currently going through something deeply painful.

You may have wounds that are wide open and feel like they will never heal. Maybe you felt like you were healing and then something happened to rip right through the scab that had formed. Maybe you feel healed but still have scars that are evidence of your wounds. Or, maybe you're numb and have no idea what you feel.

Wherever you are on your journey, being sorrowful is okay. So are tears. And I'm not the only one who says that. God says so too.

Another thing I want to say is that being heartbroken isn't a sin. Too many times we act like having faith means we're always supposed to be happy no matter what's going on. It's true that joy is accessible to us when we're following God.

But that doesn't mean we're robots with no feelings. Jesus mourned too.

Grief can be debilitating. It takes away your will to function and there's no way you can stop it. You just have to wrestle with it.

Something no one tells you is that praying doesn't take away the pain and neither does reading the Bible.

They don't take away the nauseous feeling in your stomach that you could throw up at any time, or make your head stop hurting from crying.

They don't take away feeling like you're living in an alternate universe that doesn't make sense, and you're not quite sure what the rules are or that they even exist at all.

They don't take away the questions of if you'll ever be whole again, if your heart will ever stop feeling like a rock in your chest, or if your smile will ever come back naturally.

Nope. You still have to endure all of those emotions and feel the weight of all of those uncertainties.

What prayer does do is acknowledge that God is there with you - and has always been there - waiting for you to acknowledge Him.

Reading the Bible reminds you exactly who it is you have sitting next to you, and what He says about where you are.

He doesn't stop it or fix it. After all, He didn't even bend the rules of the universe to save Himself the pain when Jesus died.

But He will be there. Comforting. Always saying the right thing. And Him being there makes it bearable. Barely at times, but bearable.

With grief, there's no rushing it. You don't feel better until you do, and then better still isn't the old "normal." It'll be a new normal though. Life will still have its beautiful moments because with God, we can always hope.

We can find beauty in the pain. For now, let's see what God says about going through grief.

A STUDY ON GRIEF

Please read each Scripture before you read each devotional.
God's words are more important than mine.

JOHN 11:33-35, PSALM 147:3

The day I wrote this, I was a mess.

The day before, I barely wrote anything. I tried - forcing myself to get out of bed and sit at my writing desk - but my mind was clouded with grief and I didn't have the words.

So I got up the next morning and went to a coffee shop to write. Good coffee in an oversized mug, my favorite orange cranberry muffin and good vibes were a sure recipe for creativity. Except that when I got there, I still felt miserable.

There I was, sitting at a table, tearing up as I wrote this, hoping the girl across from me didn't notice and think I was weird. And I still wanted to go home, get in bed and clear my schedule for the evening so I didn't have to talk to anyone.

So I did. I removed the pressure to do anything but be with Jesus that day. I didn't even make myself talk. I said, "Ok Jesus, here we are." And literally sat there.

In this passage, when Jesus saw the people around Him crying, He was deeply moved by their tears to the point that he wept too. Jesus wasn't only crying because of Lazarus' death. He was also crying because the people who loved Lazarus were suffering.

He feels the same way about us when we're hurting. God promises to be that person who sits with us. Any time, anywhere, and under any circumstance. Especially when our hearts are broken.

People say that time heals all wounds. But if you break your finger and do nothing but wait for it to heal, it won't. Because time doesn't heal wounds. It just relocates the symptoms. God is the one who heals.

As you bring your wounds to God, Jesus will meet you in your pain. He is moved by your tears and will cry with you, even when you want to cry alone. He doesn't think you're weak or weird for feeling. He felt and wept to show you it was okay.

Lean into Him and let Him comfort you.

CHALLENGE:

Bring your deepest wounds to God. Sit with Him. Cry.
And when you're ready to talk, let Him listen.

REVELATION 21:3-5

"The party is in Heaven."

I only watch movies that end in "happily ever after." Seriously. All my friends know that.

One time, I went to see "A Star is Born" with a group of friends - spoiler alert - and I was distraught afterward. I literally turned to my friend who had already seen the movie and said, "Do you even know me?" I was genuinely confused about why she would let me see that movie.

I feel like it's pointless to watch movies that remind me not every ending is a happy one because there are enough of those reminders in our real, everyday lives.

Kristin always says, "The party is in Heaven." A lot of times when discouraging things happen our first reaction is to ask why. And that's the answer. Because the real party is in Heaven and we're not there yet.

While it's true that life can be fulfilling and joyful here because of God's grace to us, "happily ever after" is for Hollywood and Heaven. This life is for purpose and holiness, so we're prepared to spend eternity with God.

That's why I love this passage. When I'm in the middle of grief, all I want is for the pain to stop and the reason I'm feeling it to be gone. And here is God's promise of that.

In Heaven, we get a fresh start where negative experiences and emotions don't even exist. There will be no more death, mourning, crying, or pain. We'll love and enjoy every moment of every day for the rest of eternity. What a hopeful state of being to look forward to.

Cheers to "happily ever after" in Heaven. Let's make sure we get there together.

CHALLENGE:

Let the vision that God promises in Heaven give you hope when you feel hopeless.

"HAPPILY EVER AFTER" IS FOR HOLLYWOOD AND HEAVEN

WEAKNESS ISN'T WEAK.

ECCLESIASTES 3:1-4, MATTHEW 5:4

There is always time.

When Daddy died, several people around me told me, "You need to take the time to mourn." And even though I wasn't trying to be disrespectful, I said, "Who has time for that?" quickly followed by, "What does that even look like?"

Crying wasn't going to bring Daddy back. We were in the middle of a pandemic and as an entrepreneur figuring out different ways to make money, I didn't have time to sit and be sad for an undetermined amount of time. No one was going to pay my bills while I "mourned." So exactly what did that mean? I needed practicals.

Then one day, I was in my closet praying and I started crying. My first instinct was to wipe my tears away immediately. I started to, but I stopped myself because that was it. I understood what they meant by taking the time to mourn.

Mourning is not drying our tears before we've finished crying them. It's not catching them before they fall. Mourning is not shaming ourselves or trying to clean up our feelings before we fully experience them.

The word mourning means deep sorrow, not just a normal "I'm sad." It's allowing yourself to be passionately sorrowful because that's how you feel, regardless of everything else going on.

There is a time for mourning and God promises to be there during it, ready and waiting to comfort you.

He can take your tears, your rage, your questions, your depression. He can take it all. He doesn't want you to feel like you have to be "happy" and put together to come to Him. He doesn't need your attempted strength or perfection.

Go to God with your full humanity, even in the hardest times. Joy will come, but not without taking the time to mourn.

CHALLENGE:

Don't try to get yourself together so you can go to God. Go to Him with everything you're feeling and figure it out together. Take the time.

PSALM 73:23-26

You never know when it'll hit you.

I was on the way to serve at a blood drive that my church was putting on. It was my first community service event since moving to San Diego this year, so I was excited. But when I arrived at the location, I recognized it.

To my surprise, it was the same hospital Daddy had been at, where we had stayed with him for five days.

The prayer walks I had taken around the hospital grounds, begging God to save him, immediately came to mind. I had never cried there though. I didn't allow it when Daddy was alive.

Pulling in that day, I lost it. One minute I was singing old school Brandy as I danced in my seat. The next, I was sobbing and shaking uncontrollably as I struggled to breathe.

It happened so unexpectedly that I stopped in the middle of the parking lot to get control of myself so I didn't hit something.

I parked and cried for 30 minutes. At one point I was desperate to be comforted by God but I couldn't feel Him. So I said, "God, I can't feel You, but I know You're here, so thank You."

That prayer helped me breathe easier and rest in my sorrow because it was a reminder to myself that I did know He was there. I wouldn't have been able to pray that before this year. But at that moment, it was true.

His Word said He was with me whether I felt Him or not. That I had known before. When I said it that day, I knew it because in my grief He'd proven it every day for the last six months.

In times like those, there's nothing we can do to fix our situation, take the hurt away, or make it not real. All we can do is acknowledge that God is near.

That's also the beautiful thing about ugly moments. We learn that God being there, holding us by our hand, is enough.

This passage reminds us of that. There's not a time when God isn't with you. Always means always. Even when your heart feels broken, or like it's going to explode because the feelings are too much, God is the strength of your heart.

In our weakness, God is our strength. And while everything else in life is temporary, His presence is not. God wants to be your counsel and your inheritance, in every moment, forever.

Let Him.

Thank God for always being close, holding you, guiding you, and
being your strength, even when you don't feel Him.

GOD IS THE STRENGTH OF MY HEART

GOD IS THE STRENGTH OF MY HEART

GOD IS THE STRENGTH OF MY HEART

GOD IS THE STRENGTH OF MY HEART

GOD IS THE STRENGTH OF MY HEART

CREATED TO WORSHIP

PSALM 59:16-17

This day was seven years ago but I can picture it like yesterday.

Kristin had just called to tell me she was in the hospital. The doctors had diagnosed her with sepsis - toxins in her blood - and were very worried. Being a TV news anchor since college, I'd never heard her strong voice sound so frail as she fought to breathe through the pain.

I was driving on the 281 freeway in Houston at the time and when we got off the phone, I broke down in tears.

Kristin and I had been best friends since I was 18 months old when she was born. My eyes water at even the thought of losing her and with that news, it was a real possibility. I immediately started praying.

I told God that I didn't think I could live without her so if He had anything else for me to do in this life, I needed her to live. Then I turned on a song called, "Say Amen," by Finding Favour. It's about reminding yourself what God has already done to help you believe He can do it again.

I turned the volume to the max and I sang as loud as I could to God as tears streamed down my face. At that moment, worshiping the God I serve helped me focus on who He'd proven Himself to be. It reminded me, especially in singing that song, of His resume of love in my life.

Sometimes, all you can do is cry. And then maybe you can pray. But if you can do anything else, worship. Because singing isn't strictly for God. It's also for us.

Worshipping reminds us of who God is, and all the reasons He can be trusted as our safe place to run to in times of trouble.

So when you're in a situation and don't know the outcome, or you're feeling a lot, or even when you need more faith to believe, do what this passage says. Sing of His love. Sing of His track record. Sing of His character. Sing of His protection.

Worship to live by faith and build your faith at the same time.

CHALLENGE:

Put together a playlist of songs that really resonate with you so you can worship God no matter what's going on.

JOHN 1:1-5

I didn't want Jesus until I read this Scripture.

One day, in a conversation with my friend Willie, he told me that if I ever wanted to start reading the Bible, to start in John. He said because the Gospel of John shows Jesus' heart the most.

Fast forward a few years to when I was finally ready to start reading, I remembered his advice. This was the first passage I had read in the Bible in years.

It grabbed my attention right away because it started off with Jesus' power and identity as God and the Word. But then it made a fundamental statement about His relationship with darkness.

Until then I had lived a life that was shiny on the outside but felt consistently dark on the inside. And at that point, I'd just gone through a messy, public breakup, a betrayal, and my basketball career was completely up in the air. My life was even darker than usual.

So when I read that Jesus was the light, that He shines in the dark, and the darkness will not over-come His light, the implications clicked right away.

It was like, "Ok. If I feel darkness inside, Jesus is the light and He's more powerful than the dark, then I need to somehow find a way to get Him inside me where this darkness is."

I got it. I didn't know exactly how to do that yet. But it was enough to keep me reading the Bible so I could learn more about this Jesus who was bigger than the dark.

Years later, after falling in love with Him, John 1:5 is still my favorite verse in the entire Bible. I have a tattoo of it on my arm so I never forget the characteristic that drew me to Jesus in the first place.

No matter what you're going through or how dark it feels, it's not darker than the light Jesus brings. Have you done everything you can to shine Jesus' light in the darkest areas of your life?

He's the only light that has not been and won't ever be overcome by the dark.

CHALLENGE:

Don't settle for things that claim to be the light but are not.
Choose the true light in Jesus daily.

THE LIGHT IN THE DARKNESS THE LIGHT IN THE DARKNESS THE LIGHT IN THE DARKNESS THE LIGHT IN THE DARKNESS THE LIGHT IN THE DARKNESS THE LIGHT IN THE DARKNESS THE LIGHT IN THE DARKNESS THE LIGHT IN THE DARKNESS THE LIGHT IN THE DARKNESS THE LIGHT IN THE DARKNESS THE LIGHT IN THE DARKNESS THE LIGHT IN THE DARKNESS THE LIGHT IN THE DARKNESS THE LIGHT IN THE DARKNESS THE LIGHT IN THE DARKNESS THE LIGHT IN THE DARKNESS THE LIGHT IN THE DARKNESS THE LIGHT IN THE DARKNESS THE LIGHT IN THE DARKNESS

I KINGS 19:9-18

Grief has taught me to accept that I'm breakable.

For the first week after Daddy died, my friend and roommate, Lee, would come home and ask, "Did you eat today?" Or she'd just order food and bring it to me. When someone knows your Chipotle order without asking, that's a real friend.

It was frustrating because I didn't want to be laying there, crying and unable to move. I wanted to be productive, and be able to figure it out and suck it up. But I couldn't. I physically didn't have the ability to.

Even now, one day I'll be speaking at an event in front of hundreds of people and the next it'll be hard for me to get out of bed and talk to anyone. That's how unpredictable grief is. I can go from powerful to fragile quickly and without warning.

Normally I'd beat myself up for that. But during this time, God has taught me how I should be treated. He's been so gentle with me.

This passage is encouraging for a couple of different reasons. First, in the chapter before - I absolutely recommend you read it - Elijah had a showdown with 450 false prophets. He called down fire from Heaven and proved without a doubt that they were worshipping false gods. It was epic.

So the fact that we see him hiding in a cave and depressed in the very next chapter reminds me that even the boldest, strongest, most spiritual people have moments when they don't always exude those characteristics. Definitely comforting.

Then there's how God handled the situation. When God found Elijah hiding in the cave, He knew it wasn't because Elijah didn't want to do the right thing. On the contrary, Elijah wanted to keep going. He was just discouraged, hopeless, overwhelmed, lonely and beat up. So God came to Elijah gently, with a solution to his problems.

I think more often than not, we set unrealistic standards for ourselves instead of allowing our humanity. Then we expect God to treat us how we treat ourselves. But just like in this passage, instead of appearing forcefully like the wind, an earthquake, or a fire, God comes to us in a gentle whisper.

Whether you're feeling like Elijah in chapter 18 or chapter 19, God is here for you. Don't be afraid of Him being harsh or forceful in your weak moments.

God knows everyone has them and isn't here to kick you when you're down. He's here to take care of you, gently.

God knows how to be gentle when you're hurting. Take His lead
and speak to yourself gently also.

THE STRONG ARE ALLOWED TO BE WEAK

HEBREWS 5:7-9

I wasn't the person I needed to be yet.

God, What the Heck?! is actually my second book. In my first book about confidence, I shared many of my own opinions and if I'm being honest, it wasn't that hard to write.

With this one, I had no idea what I was getting myself into. Writing a book including Scripture meant that I didn't just have to believe the Scriptures, or even simply have strong convictions on them. I needed the heart to communicate in a way that helps people understand and apply the Word of God to their lives.

I thought I had that heart when I decided to write a devotional book three years ago. But I was wrong. That heart had to be developed along the way and grows every day.

To facilitate that, God had to allow my heart to break so I could speak to those who are broken-hearted with empathy. And He had to build my faith so I could openly share with others without fear.

Because I wasn't secure enough in God's protection to be vulnerable with people who could hurt me. I was too numb to feel my own wounds and therefore too detached to safeguard anyone else's. And I didn't see my need for help so I felt inconvenienced by others who needed it.

I was strong, independent, and although that's been beneficial at times, it was also standing in the way of me being fully obedient to God's call of loving people.

It was my suffering and willingness to submit to God, even when it felt like torture, that helped me become a person who is capable of both obedience and the life calling that comes with it.

I definitely haven't arrived on this one. I'm learning more about how to do what God has called me to do every day. But I'm on the way there.

This passage of Scripture shows one of my favorite things about Jesus in that He never asks us to do anything He hasn't already done. Jesus embodied God's standards by living them out.

But even though He was God in the flesh, in His humanity, Jesus still had to be made into the person who could fulfill the assignment God had for Him. It was through His suffering that He impacted the entire world.

Even in your lowest, most painful times, God is trying to birth something in you. There are character traits, knowledge, and temperaments that can only come from suffering. And whatever your call is, it will be incomplete at best and impossible at worst without complete reliance and submission to God in the process.

Just like Jesus' suffering led the way for others, and I believe mine will too, so will yours.

CHALLENGE:

Follow Jesus' example. Pray passionately in times of suffering, and submit your heart to being obedient so that God can use your life to its fullest.

SOMETIMES GOD CALLS YOU TO DO SOMETHING AND THEN MAKES YOU INTO THE PERSON WHO CAN DO IT.

PASS IT ON.

2 CORINTHIANS 1:3-4

Empathy is a superpower born out of grief.

Last year I was invited to be one of the co-hosts on Melyssa Ford's podcast, "I'm Here For The Food." After eight episodes, we decided it wasn't a good fit and parted ways.

About six months later and a month after Daddy died, I saw a video about Melyssa's mom dying also. Even though we hadn't talked since I left the show, I immediately reached out to her.

I didn't know grief before this season and I'm not the world's most empathetic person. Not even close. I've had many people around me lose loved ones before this and I never knew what to say. But this time I did.

I was able to relate, comfort, pass on a book that helped me, and film another podcast episode about the grief process. A silver lining about losing some-one so close to me was that it helped me learn how to be there for people.

The word for comfort in Greek - the original language this passage was written in - means a personal, intimate urging or calling to one's aid.[2] God personally and intimately comes to our aid in times of need, allowing us to do the same for others.

One of the best parts of God's comfort is that we get to pass it on.

There are times we feel like we have nothing to give people, the world, even ourselves. But as we share our experiences with others, God will give us the ability to empathize without being overwhelmed. The goal is that as God comes to our aid in our worst circumstances, others will be inspired to turn to Him in theirs.

We can add "all comfort" to the long list of God's character traits we've already discussed. All comfort for all troubles. That means there isn't one thing you've been through, are going through, or will ever go through that God can't comfort you in the middle of.

All means all. Keep turning to God instead of away from Him and you will have more than enough to help others do the same.

CHALLENGE:

When you're ready, seek out conversations with people who are going through the same things and share what you're learning about God's love.

1 SAMUEL 30:3-8

God gives the best pep talks.

We were playing a huge game against our college rival, Tennessee, but it didn't start out well. I picked up a couple of early fouls and spent too much of the first half on the bench. Thankfully, my teammates played well and it was still a close game when we went into half time.

As soon as I walked into the locker room, Coach Gaudet pulled me over to the side so I could vent my frustrations to him before going to sit with my team. He was calm and reassured me that we had a lot of basketball left to play.

Then he said I had a decision to make. Was I going to be the kind of leader my team could count on in our biggest moments? Or was I going to flake on them when they needed me most? Without hesitation, I chose the first kind of leader. "Good," he replied.

Then we rejoined the team to hear Coach Foster's strategy for how we were going to win the game. And that's exactly what we did.

Here we see a similar method with David and his men. When faced with a horrible situation - much graver than the possibility of losing a basketball game - they wept until they had no strength left. As he wept, David found comfort and strength in God. God gave him the hug and the pep talk he needed to keep going.

After he was strengthened, he got his game plan and followed it to victory. The Bible gives us a simple, perfect process on how to get through a painful circumstance.

We've talked about this throughout this chapter. Be raw and honest as you tell God exactly how you're feeling and seek comfort from Him. Take the time to do it on purpose and He will be whatever you need.

Resolve not to stay in a state of mourning though. There is still a time for everything. Get direction from God. Find Scriptures that relate to what you need and ask advice from people who follow Him. If you don't know anyone who can help you with the Scriptures, ask God to send someone. He'll do that too.

Then go do what God said. It won't be neat because grief never is. It may feel more like cycles than stages and that's ok. But continue repeating the process as often as you need. God is right there.

There is a time to mourn and take as much time as you need. There is also much life left to live and God wants to use you, even in your grief, beyond what you can imagine. He is there, to give you comfort, strength, and unlimited pep talks.

Weep, find strength, get direction, execute, repeat.

GOD GIVES THE BEST PEP TALKS

6. No

SHAME

(A Conversation About Overcoming Shame)

AND SO CALLING FOR HELP WAS
TELLING OUR SECRET...

Shame - a painful emotion caused by consciousness of guilt, shortcoming, or impropriety[3]

Shame affects every single one of us.

After my parents' divorce and the move back to Southern California, Mommy wasn't in the best shape to take care of us. Before the divorce, she'd been diagnosed with a mental illness. I'm sure leaving her college sweetheart and taking care of three kids alone didn't help.

As things escalated from difficult to neglectful to abusive, Kristin and I fought all of our battles together.

One time, we locked ourselves in our room with Mommy outside, beating on the door and demanding we let her in. Instead we moved the dresser in front of the door in case the lock didn't hold.

I told Kristin to yell out of the window for help. She opened the window and said, "Help," too quietly for anyone to hear. I said, "Kristin, yell louder!"

She looked at me with fear in her eyes like she didn't want to. And even though we did need help, I understood how she was feeling. We had both worked really hard to keep our home life hidden from everyone, even Daddy, so calling for help was telling our secret.

That's what shame does. It makes you hide things, even when it would be in your best interest to share them. I remember a lot of shameful moments as a child, and our shame as children turns into shame as adults.

We can feel it in so many ways:
Past abuse
Finances
Never doing "enough"
Appearance
Mental illness
Sexual assault
Sexual history
Sexual performance
Having feelings
Feeling feelings
Not feeling feelings
Giving in to feelings

Not being perfect
Saying the "wrong" thing
Hurting someone
Being rejected
Failing
Asking for help
Accepting help
Not helping
Not being "successful"

The list could go on.

Shame is crippling. When we feel it, it's because we've internalized a belief that something we did or that happened made us unlovable, and that if people found out they wouldn't want anything to do with us. Them deserting us would further prove, in our mind, the "truth" of our worthlessness.

Since unfailing love is the one thing we're all seeking, that belief that we're unlovable becomes our secret, causing us to hide from people, from ourselves, and ultimately from God.

When we hide, nothing heals.

The problem multiplies and spreads to different areas of our lives, likely damaging our relationships the most. It prevents us from allowing people close because in every interaction we're trying to protect our secret so they'll stay and not leave.

Shame stops us from empowering people to love us.

We might not say out loud, "I'm probably feeling shame about this." But if we're intentionally covering up details about our past or our actions, there's a good chance it's attached.

It all starts with doing your best as you go through life. When something discouraging happens, Satan - or someone repeating what Satan has told him or her - comes along and starts whispering things in your ear like, "you're not good enough, you're a failure, they'll never love you, and you deserved that."

With every word and every step, you believe that voice more and more, eventually repeating the words to yourself every time anything isn't perfect. Life eventually becomes a conversation between you, Satan's lies, and others who replay them back to you.

So what I want to do with this chapter is draw you into a different conversation.

You and I are going to talk about life and shame, and we're going to replace Satan's words with God's.

The challenge is, instead of allowing the narrative you've been internalizing to feed the shame, commit to having a conversation that's healing.

Let's study it out.

WHEN

WE

HIDE,

NOTHING

HEALS.

A STUDY ON SHAME

Please read each Scripture before you read each devotional.
God's words are more important than mine.

JESUS COVERS YOUR SHAME

GENESIS 2:25, 3:8-10

We were created to be shameless.

When I'm not feeling confident, I go to my sister's Instagram page to look at pictures of my niece, Phoenix aka Missy, so I can imitate her.

She just turned four and is the cutest, most confident and carefree little girl - I could be a little biased. She wears whatever she wants, whether it's a princess dress or an outfit with seven colors and three patterns. She dances when her favorite Trolls movie comes on, no matter who's watching. Anything she says or does is good enough for her so it's good enough for everyone else.

That's how we were made to be. Just like children have no shame, neither did Adam and Eve. Because God didn't create us to walk in shame.

The first appearance we see of shame is when sin entered the world. Before Adam and Eve disobeyed God, they felt no shame when they were naked. After they sinned, they hid and clothed themselves, showing us that they were ashamed of their sin and nakedness.

As Adam and Eve hid from God in fear of His response and disapproval, He called out and went looking for them. Even though He didn't agree with what they'd done and allowed them to suffer the consequences, He also covered their shame by giving them clothes.

It's interesting that the animal God sacrificed for their clothes to cover their shame is a foreshadowing of Jesus being sacrificed to cover our sin. It's incredible how the Bible repeats the same principles over and over again.

Just like Adam and Eve, we feel shame when we know we've done something wrong. Or, when we believe we've done or participated in something that won't be seen as right.

Regardless of what happened, God doesn't want you to live shamefully, or to hide in it. He'll come looking for you and when He does, He wants you to come out from where you're hiding. His deepest desire is to take away your shame through Jesus and continue walking with you through whatever comes out of it.

God won't abandon you no matter what you've done. He wants to free you from your shame.

CHALLENGE:

What are you trying to hide from God that you feel shameful for? Talk to Him about it instead.

CLEAN OUT THE SKELETONS.

JOHN 3:16-21

Walking in the light can be scary.

I got an STD when I was in college. That's probably not something you expected to read in a devotional book but we're talking about shame, so here we go.

When I started having symptoms I was scared that it was a serious issue and ashamed to have gotten anything in the first place. Even Googling my symptoms to find out what I had felt embarrassing. It's not something people usually talk about openly, even though it's pretty common, and at that point I wanted to ignore it and hide.

Instead, I went and got checked. Walking into the clinic to talk to the doctor, I felt exposed. But being there was the only way for me to get better.

Thankfully I caught it immediately and it was curable. I did recognize that it could've easily not been, and for maybe the first time realized I wasn't immune to the cost of my actions.

You might be thinking, "Wow, Chantelle, I can't believe you just told me that." It is relatively personal. Still, I'm not scared to share about who I was and the things I did before Jesus because there's no more shame attached to it.

Jesus came to set us free from condemnation. First though, we have to be willing to be exposed.

Even the word "exposed" is uncomfortable. We have to do it though. Just like I wasn't going to be cured without telling the doctor what was going on, we have to tell God. It should be easy because He already knows, yet for some reason, it's not.

There are times we know we're doing wrong. And if we don't know when we're doing it, the consequences show us afterward. We can be so ashamed that we hide in the dark instead of stepping into the light to get the help we need.

Shame is something we all deal with because we all sin. We all have skeletons in our closet and it's dark in there. Jesus is the light that will overcome the dark, but the light isn't selective. It exposes everything.

When you can see everything, you know where to heal.

It's time to let go of any fear you have of being exposed and open up to God so He can help you heal.

CHALLENGE:

Be honest with God about something you're ashamed of. Ask Him to
help you stop hiding so you can get the help you need.

MATTHEW 27:1-5

At the end of high school and two weeks before college, I was raped. I was so ashamed that instead of telling anyone, I privately chastised myself for the next year, watching my self-esteem plummet as well.

When I finally did get up the guts to tell a friend he said, "You're a big girl. You could've stopped it if you wanted to."

I was devastated. At the time I believed the rape was my fault and in my mind, his comment proved me right, which sent me even deeper into the shame hole I was in.

When I got to college men became a game to me. I manipulated them every chance I got, determined to control them for that one time I couldn't control that one man. My obsession with control would end up hurting so many people, me included. And the whole time I hated myself for it.

It wasn't until I was able to work through my shame with Jesus in the Scriptures that things started to be different.

Shame will eat you alive from the inside if you let it.

And there's no better example of that in the Bible than Judas.

Even though Judas betrayed Jesus, he eventually realized the gravity of what he did. He understood and he was broken because of it. But the way he handled his sorrow ended in suicide.

Judas could've gone to Jesus because Jesus would have forgiven him. He could've gone to people who knew Jesus because they would have pointed him back to Jesus.

But instead, he tried to fix it himself. In his genuine remorse, he went to people who didn't understand the depth of Jesus' love and forgiveness. And it killed him.

For us, maybe this looks like an eventual physical death. Or it can look like us dying spiritually along with everything that God wants to do through us. Can you imagine how powerful Judas' story of repentance would have been?

God wants you to know that there's no reason to go anywhere else for resolution. He will always forgive you, no matter what you've done. There is nothing too shameful for Him to heal, but trying to heal it on your own is not the answer.

When you want to make something you've done right, go to Jesus and people who will point you back to Jesus. That's the only way you'll know what else should come next.

GO TO JESUS.

2 CORINTHIANS 7:8-12

Feel it but don't stay there.

There are two common ways athletes respond when they make a mistake.

The first player pats her chest and says, "my bad." She does it to tell her team she knows she messed up. It's a quick way to take accountability. Sometimes she'll wear a rubber band on her wrist and snap it to help her feel the pain of her mistake.

Then she moves on, trying her hardest to correct whatever she did wrong. Her mantra is, "Next play."

The second player says, "my bad." She knows it was her fault too. But instead of moving on, she lets the mistake get in her head. She keeps beating herself up for it and ends up losing her confidence.

Because of that, for the rest of the game she can't make any of the plays she would normally make. Her mantra is, "Why do I suck?"

We can be like this in life too. No one is perfect so we'll always be tempted to feel shame. Whether or not we do depends on how we interpret our mistakes. It's the difference between godly sorrow and worldly sorrow.

Worldly sorrow causes you to beat yourself up, justify your actions or even blame others. It makes you want to give up or lash out. As the Scripture says, "worldly sorrow brings death."

With godly sorrow, feeling the pain of what you did wrong can still be devastating. But in place of giving up or lashing out, you focus on moving forward and doing better.

When we're feeling worldly sorrow, we'll look back in shame at what we can't change instead of looking forward to what we can.

The goal is to be the first type of player in life. Identify your mistakes because that's the only way to get better. God doesn't want you to be discouraged by them though. That doesn't do anyone any good.

Instead, when you see your mistakes, feel an earnestness, eagerness, indignation, alarm, longing, concern, and a readiness to make it right. God wants the type of sorrow that moves you towards action.

Don't get stuck in any sorrow that comes from shame. Change and move forward.

Is your sorrow leading you to shame or to action? Focus on what you can do to make it right and move on to the next play in every situation.

2 CORINTHIANS 12:6-10

Its purpose is to keep you close to God.

There wasn't much pure about my life before Jesus. And definitely not my relationships. I was crude in my speech, watched porn, had sex outside of marriage and set zero boundaries in friendships.

Society tells me that behavior is fine but the Bible says differently. So when I chose Jesus, I stopped doing those things. But that doesn't take away the experiences, the memories or even the desires.

Sometimes I struggle to keep my mind where God wants it to be. I may unintentionally look at someone and think a sexually impure thought about them. Or remember an experience from the past and entertain that memory instead of forcing myself to think about something else.

Then I'll put my head in my hands like, "No, get out!" I despise the fact that I have those desires and the past experience to bring them to life in the first place.

But I've had to learn not to shame myself for that. The past is the past and there's nothing wrong with me. It's just an area where I'm weak and need more of God's strength.

This passage is interesting because Paul had something about himself that he wanted to change too. He called it, "a thorn in his flesh." He kept begging for God to take it away and God refused.

The answer was "no" because if Paul didn't have that thorn, he would think too highly of himself and be tempted not to rely on God. God had given him so much talent, experience and intellect that He had to make sure Paul always realized his need.

We all have thorns in our flesh. It's the thing you've been trying to change on your own forever but can't. Or the thing God's Word is telling you to give up but you don't want to. Our thorns may be different but we all have them.

You'll have times, as I still do, when you'll give in to your thorn and are tempted to beat yourself up for it. Yet God's grace is enough for those times, and His strength is enough to make you strong in your weakness.

There are some aspects of your character that will never completely go away. But God will give you the ability to overcome them daily.

Instead of getting disappointed or shaming yourself, thank God. Because the weakness keeping you close to Him might be the thing that saves your soul.

CHALLENGE:

Identify your thorn. Then pray and trust that God will give you His strength to obey and His grace when you fall.

HIS GRACE IS SUFFICIENT.

CREATE IN ME A PURE HEART, OH GOD

PSALM 51:10-17

I gave God my platform before I had one.

At the beginning of my relationship with God, I was reading the Bible, really trying to understand, get to know Him and fall in love. It took me a while to build that kind of relationship with Him.

Once I did, I understood that the life I was living before didn't make God proud, which was the whole point of Him giving it to me. My behavior had hurt a lot of people and made it harder for them to find Him. I had been living the opposite of what God wanted.

The thing that convicted me the most, though, was that God had given me talent and influence for a big part of my adult life. And instead of using any of it for Him, I had used all of it for myself, to hurt people. That broke me.

At that moment I told God, "I'm so sorry. I just want to be right with You. I don't need a title. I don't need to have any kind of platform. I'll just follow. But God, if You choose to give me another platform, whatever that looks like I promise to use it for You." When I said amen, I didn't care what God did with that prayer. I was just grateful that I finally knew the truth.

Since then, I've had small platforms and considerably larger ones. But no matter who was looking and listening it was my goal to show them Jesus.

I can relate to David's prayer in this passage. He was an adulterer and a murderer whose heart was shattered because of his sin. He knew he couldn't take back or change anything he'd done. But he was coming to God with sorrow and humility to ask for forgiveness.

David asked God to create in him a pure heart, meaning he knew he didn't currently have one.

The right heart before God isn't necessarily pure. It's honest. We must come to Him with a heart sober about where we are and committed to giving our best efforts to change that.

God wants your heart. He can make it pure. And when you offer it to Him there's nothing you've done in the past that will make Him turn it away.

CHALLENGE:

Pray David's prayer to God, personalizing it where needed. Ask
Him to change your heart to be what He wants it to be.

"ME TOO."
— JESUS

HEBREWS 4:14-16

Being understood is comforting.

The other day one of the young ladies I spiritually mentor said, "Chan, I love that when I come to you with something I've done wrong, you don't freak out. You're so gentle with me."

Hearing that instantly made my day because that is definitely a new aspect of my character, courtesy of the last two years.

I have learned many great lessons from sports but empathy and gentleness were not among them. When you play sports it's like, "I understand you're crying but you have a game in ten minutes so get out of your feelings and go perform." The only thing that mattered was winning and if I didn't win no one cared why.

So when someone else came to me for sympathy, I spoke to them with the same tone I spoke to myself: "Get out of your feelings and figure it out." Unfortunately, it rarely helped them feel loved, get out of their feelings or figure anything out. I wasn't trying to hurt them but I genuinely couldn't relate.

So I started praying for compassion and God reminded me what it was like to feel broken. It was painful, but it taught me how to treat people gently because I could relate to the need for gentleness.

Pain is the price we pay for compassion.

That's one of the reasons I love this Scripture. Jesus treats us with grace and mercy because He's God, but also because He can relate to our feelings. He's been sad, upset, tormented, hungry, insulted, disrespected, and anything else we can possibly feel.

Jesus can also relate to every temptation we've ever struggled with that comes with those feelings. Even though He never sinned, He still knows how hard it is not to. He understands. That's why we don't have to be scared to go to Him. He's not going to judge us for feeling the way we feel, or being imperfect.

Jesus is ready to give you mercy for when you mess up and the grace of another chance. So pray with confidence. He gets it and He's there to help.

CHALLENGE:

When you're tempted to be afraid of how Jesus will respond,
remember He can relate. Expect grace and mercy instead.

LUKE 7:36-48

What they think of you is between them and Jesus.

There was this guy I semi-dated in college who I kept in touch with after graduation. One day we were having a conversation and he approached the subject of us dating again, even though we hadn't had that type of relationship in over 10 years.

When he said it, I told him that God was the foundation of my life and him not having the same belief meant dating wasn't something I was open to exploring. It wasn't meant as a judgment of his lifestyle but more as a communication of mine.

For some reason, that set him off. He was extremely upset. He started bringing up sin from my past, saying that if the people at my church knew who I really was they'd kick me out. He called me fake and said a lot of other things that were completely inappropriate.

I was like, "Wow, that escalated quickly." I mean, everything he said about my past was true. But it was the past.

As I was listening to him, I was shocked and tempted to feel shame. Some of the things he brought up I hadn't thought about in years. It was a conscious decision for me to stand strong in the moment and not let him get to me.

This is why I admire the woman in this story so much.

She was infamous and her reputation didn't just appear out of thin air. It was accurately based on the life she'd been living. But it allowed her to see her need for Jesus. She sought Him out and showed that she was ready to be different through her deep love and sacrifice.

It took a lot of courage to crash the party of a modern-day religious leader as an outcast with a shady past. But she did it because she was desperate to get right with God.

We don't know if she worried about what other people would think or say. I imagine she probably did, at least a little bit. Either way, we do know that it didn't stop her.

The conversation that mattered was between her and Jesus.

That's how it needs to be for us. Anyone who will shame us for our pasts by throwing it in our faces isn't important. Anyone who refuses to believe our efforts to change are sincere is inconsequential.

This journey is about you and Christ. Imitate this woman. Persevere through anyone's attempts to shame you and sit at Jesus' feet, crying there if you have to.

Jesus doesn't care if you have a past. For Him, no one is beyond saving. No one is too far gone for a fresh start. And His is the only opinion that matters.

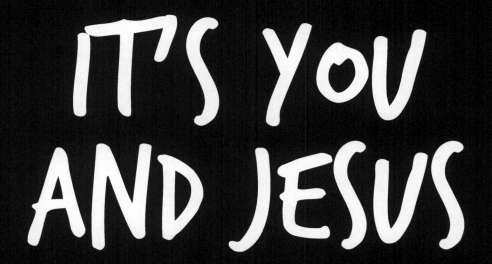

IT'S YOU AND JESUS

YOUR BEST IS GOOD ENOUGH YOUR BEST IS GOOD ENOUGH

1 PETER 5:6-7

Exhale and let go of it all.

When I first wrote this, it was 8:52 at night. So far that day, I had slept, cried and eaten. And that was enough.

The day before was six months since I lost Daddy. I actually felt myself getting sad all week leading up to it but I was right in the middle of planning a Singles Ministry Conference for five churches. I didn't exactly have time to be in my feelings, so I wasn't.

But the day after the conference ended, I woke up feeling like I had a hangover. I only got out of bed for necessities.

One of my most common phrases is, "Who has time for this?" When I'm getting sick, "Who has time for this?" When I'm overwhelmed by feelings, "Who has time for this?" When I'm threatening to break down and desperately need self-care, "Who has time for this?"

Kristin and I have a running joke that we're always trying to conquer the world, so it's hard for me to take time out of my schedule for things that don't contribute to that. Still, I've come to learn that I need to take care of myself without feeling shame about it.

That's one reason I love this passage. It feels like God said, "Chill, you good." It's permission to exhale the pressure we put on ourselves to be perfect, let go of the shame that comes with those expectations, and place all that anxiety on God instead.

To be humble is to accurately see yourself relative to God and acknowledge your need for Him. That means stop expecting yourself to have your superhero cape on all the time. You're human.

Even when you're not overachieving and taking over the world, as long as you're willing to humble yourself before God, not trying to play His role, He will lift you up at the right time.

Some days your best looks different than other days. And there's no shame in that. If you'll let God be God in your life and walk with Him daily, He'll take your anxiety and replace it with grace, mercy, love, and strength.

CHALLENGE:

Acknowledge your need for God and don't beat yourself up for not always living up to your own expectations.

EPHESIANS 3:14-19, 1 JOHN 4:18

It always goes back to love.

Whenever I got off the phone with Daddy, I would say, "I love you!" And he would always say, "I love you more."

Even though He joked about a lot, he never said that in an excited or funny way. It was always a matter-of-fact statement like it was something that was simply true. And whenever I tried to argue with him about it, he'd tell me, "Chantelle, you don't understand."

I've heard a lot of parents say that they love their children more than the kids can understand. I thought it was just something parents said, more like a cliche. But now that I think about it, maybe it's true.

Maybe I didn't understand. Because if I really believed Daddy loved me more, I would've trusted him more, obeyed him more and talked to him about more. I would've let go of the fear keeping me from doing all of those things.

It's the same with God. Not understanding God's love sounds cliche. Until you realize that if we did, we would know that His love is simply true and that our actions will never change it. We would trust more, obey more, and run to Him more.

We wouldn't hide in shame or fear His response when we mess up. Instead, we'd remember who He is and who we are to Him. And we would never be afraid of Him loving us less.

We are each more than the worst thing we've done, and God is bigger than all of them put together.

He wants to love you anyway and He wants to love you through it. But He's not going to force you to stop hiding in shame. He won't take your free will, remember?

What He will do is continue showing His love in different ways until you decide that going through life without Him is too hard or too empty.

And when you do, He'll be right there, because He loves you. Which means you have nothing to fear and nothing to be ashamed of.

CHALLENGE:

Any time your shame makes you want to hide from God, bring it back to His love for you and go to Him anyway.

IT ALWAYS COMES BACK TO GOD'S LOVE.

7. COPING

WITH JESUS

(A Conversation About Coping)

LOOKING BACK, IT WAS THE
STRONGEST MOMENT OF MY LIFE.

One of the worst nights of my life happened 12 years ago.

I had just torn my Achilles tendon while playing professionally in Turkey. It was my second major injury in a row - I had only played three games after spending seven months rehabbing a broken knee cap - and I swore my WNBA career over.

That night I desperately wanted to escape my feelings. I was drowning. So I called my friend and said, "Hey, I need some weed." "I got you, come over," he replied.

As he was rolling the second blunt, I saw a gun on his coffee table. He saw me looking at it and asked if I had ever seen a gun in real life before. I said "no" and he handed it to me.

It was cold. Heavy. But for the first time since my injury, I felt powerful and in control. I had the power to take my own life, control over whether I lived or died.

As I pressed the barrel to my head and put my finger on the trigger, I called myself weak for not being able to pull it. I wished I could.

Looking back, it was the strongest moment of my life. But I didn't put the gun down until I left. I held on to the power for as long as I could.

We smoked again and I went home.

When I got there, I went to the freezer and drank half a bottle of vodka. Then I started to cry. That soft, violent cry that comes from so deep inside that it loses the sound on the way out.

And as I laid down on the living room floor, the last thing I remember saying was, "God, please help me."

Fast forward to 12 years later.

Daddy was in the hospital. I felt miserable, tired of constantly fighting to hope, and definitely not in control.

By that time I had become a Christian and so my previous weed-vodka cocktail wasn't an option. But that didn't stop me from wanting to numb out. All I wanted to do was eat sweets, watch movies, and sleep an embarrassing number of hours.

There were even times that I did want to go back to smoking and drinking.

Coping, though it can sometimes have a negative connotation, isn't necessarily bad. There are various definitions, most of them agreeing that it involves specific things we do to deal with and attempt to overcome problems and difficulties.[4]

So coping itself is neutral. It's not good, bad, righteous or sinful. What can become problematic are the things we cope with and the prominence we allow them in our coping process.

For example, this chapter is called, "Coping With Jesus." Going to Jesus for help in getting through difficult times is exactly what God wants us to do.

But there are many other things we can cope with that end up hurting us more than they're helping us. Those are the ones we need to stay away from.

For me, coping becomes detrimental when it's more about survival than healing.

When I try to lessen, redirect, and escape the pain so I can survive for an extended period of time without also working to heal, that's when I know I'm coping in an unhealthy way.

You may cope differently than I do but we all do it in one way or another. So I wrote this chapter to help us out. How do we prevent ourselves from coping in ways that end up crippling us more in the process? How do we cope with Jesus instead?

Let's study it out.

A STUDY ON COPING

Please read each Scripture before you read each devotional.
God's words are more important than mine.

FORTRESS
DELIVERER
REFUGE
SHIELD
STRONGHOLD

2 SAMUEL 22:1-3

The answer is always to run to God.

I first started playing basketball with the YMCA in the 7th grade. Everyone expected me to be good because I was tall, but my coordination hadn't caught up to my body yet so I was actually terrible. I was also really shy so whenever I fouled - which was often - it felt like I was getting in trouble in front of everyone. It was traumatizing.

One game, I fouled out in the first half and instead of going to sit on the bench with my teammates, I went into the stands, sat down next to my Mom and cried on her shoulder. I have no idea what the people around me thought, but it seemed like my only logical option at the time.

When I read about how David saw God, it reminds me of how obvious it was for me to run to Mom even though it might not have made sense to others.

David was a powerful, good looking, successful King and I'm sure in people's minds, fighting his battles on his own would have still been wise. But he knew he was nothing without God's help. David had so much faith that God would be whatever he needed in any situation that his default was to run to Him.

Even though David wasn't perfect by any means, he knew God was strong and secure enough to protect him.

God wants to be the first and most instinctive place we run to in any challenging circumstance. He wants to be our fortress, deliverer, refuge, shield, and stronghold just like He was for David. And it's not a coincidence that all of those words describe somewhere or something that defends you in times of great trouble. David's life wasn't all rainbows and butterflies. He went to God to get through and that's what sustained him.

When we were young we looked for someone to run to when we were hurt. Naturally, it could've been our parents or maybe a favorite teacher. Then we grew up, learned that people fail us sometimes and started trying to figure everything out ourselves.

But God won't fail you as people do. He wants you to trust that so you run to Him. And when you do, He'll be there.

CHALLENGE:

When you're stressed, angry, or hurting, before you go to anything else, pray and look up a Scripture to help first.

ISAIAH 31:1-3

I was really just trying to survive.

One morning I was writing out my prayers and I said, "God, I keep asking you to help me deal with my life but I feel like You keep taking away everything that comforts me! During the time when I need them most."

He quickly reminded me that taking away everything that made me comfortable was helping because it was forcing me to depend on Him.

I was being self-reliant in that I wasn't depending on God, but I was being codependent in that I was using other crutches to sustain me instead. He'd revealed this to me before and there I was, exposed again.

I don't think I'm the only one. A lot of us have been exposed.

Relationships that are built on sex and shallow connections get exposed.

Confidence that is built on an idea of control gets exposed.

Sanity that is built on the ability to distract ourselves from our fears gets exposed.

Our reliance on seeing celebrities as super-human gets exposed.

Identity that is built on what we do instead of who God is gets exposed.

So many things we depend on outside of God fail us. The things we count on for our provision, validation, protection and love aren't reliable. And when that happens we're suddenly aware of our lack of control.

This is why God warns us. "Woe" signifies great sorrow or distress, and Egypt in a spiritual sense represents anything in the world that's not of God. Too often in coping, we pour everything into unstable structures, trusting them to comfort, value and elevate us at a time when we're already hurting.

Only God can build and tear down. When we depend on anything but Him, it falls, and then so do we. There are many times when coping poses as survival but is really self-sabotage.

God is saying, "No, don't do it!" He doesn't want you to fail and He doesn't want you to trust in something that will fail you. He wants you to place your trust firmly in the only thing that won't fail: Himself.

Everything you were looking for in whatever got exposed, look for in God. Thank God for taking things away to allow you to see anywhere your faith was in "Egypt" more than it was in Him.

What's been exposed in your life lately? Commit to seeking God over that thing and trust that He'll come through.

DON'T LET COPING BE SELF-SABOTAGE

MATTHEW 27:32-34

Writing this book kept me from being a zombie.

After Daddy died, I wanted to numb out so that I could pass the time without hurting. But I had also started writing this book. And the thing about writing is that it's impossible to produce quality work from a genuine place if you don't actually go to that place. I couldn't write anything until I was willing to feel everything.

That's probably the best part of God's timing in this. During a situation where my numbing would have been more self-destructive than ever, I was forced to fight my natural inclination to do so at every turn.

Most times I wouldn't even realize I was numbing until I couldn't write. Then I'd be like, "Oh, I guess I have been going back and forth from Instagram to Facebook ten times without doing anything on either. I should probably stop and figure out exactly what I'm feeling."

The purpose in this writing process as a positive way to cope and bring me back to God might have saved my future self.

I'm excited to get to the point where numbing isn't my automatic first reaction and a self-correction afterwards.

In this passage of Scripture, even though Jesus was in agony on the way to be crucified, when they offered Him a drink that would have numbed the pain He refused to take it. That self-control is goals.

There are a lot of reasons God doesn't want us to numb: it makes us unproductive, places whatever we're numbing with before God, desensitizes us to the pain of others, and takes away the sober mind we need to protect ourselves and our loved ones from Satan's attacks.

We also can't selectively numb. If we numb the feelings we don't like, the feelings we crave go with it.

God wants us to feel joy, satisfaction, pleasure, and contentment, even in the midst of our trials. But so many of us can't feel happy because we've numbed away our sadness. We can't feel the satisfaction of fighting and overcoming temptations because we numbed our way through the battle.

Then we wonder why life feels either exciting or miserable with little middle ground. It's because we're too numb to feel anything other than extremes.

Follow Jesus' example by choosing not to numb. Let God help you go through your feelings. Then you'll give yourself back the ability to feel the true happiness God has for you on the other side of the pain, and even during it at times.

Trust God to carry you through your sorrow so that you can also feel your joy.

CHALLENGE:

The next time someone offers you something to numb your pain, say no. Make sure you're using your coping strategies to feel your experiences instead of running from your emotions.

FEEL THE FEELINGS.

LUKE 10:38-42, 1 CORINTHIANS 10:23

Let's talk about distractions.

The other day I took home leftovers from a restaurant and put them in the fridge for lunch the next day. Then I went grocery shopping, moved everything around, put new food in front of it and totally forgot it existed.

A couple weeks later I opened the fridge and noticed something was smelling awful. I had no idea what or where it was so I started taking things out until I got all the way back to my now rotten leftovers.

I've for sure done this with life too.

Something happens that I don't have the time, capacity, or desire to deal with at the moment. I'm "full." So I stash it away in my mind and heart, totally intending to come back and deal with it at a better time.

Except I get distracted. Issues come up. Life gets busy. I don't go back and deal with it because I don't "need" to. Or, more often, I intentionally pile on other responsibilities because I don't want to.

Then suddenly I'm overwhelmed.

In this passage, I totally get Martha. She had Jesus coming to eat at her house - Jesus! - and she needed to get it ready. Her noble heart to provide care and hospitality was amazing. But the problem was her priorities.

One of the misconceptions of coping is that we only cope with substances, people, or experiences that will obviously hurt us. Many times though, we use positive things on the outside to distract us from the work we need to do on the inside.

We choose what's more pressing, more appetizing, or just more convenient. Until it starts to show up in our lives as something else.

Mistrust...
An unexpected trigger...
Relentless ambition that's never enough...
Constant overwhelm...
An inability to accept love...

However it shows up, it starts to "smell." We start responding in ways that are bigger than what we're going through. Or maybe we're numb when we obviously should be feeling something. Either way, we're wondering where it's coming from and why.

So what are you supposed to do when this happens?

Prioritize the healing you should be doing over everything else you could be doing.

Just like the fridge, you go through your head and heart, finding the boxes that you stashed away because you didn't have time for them. You confront them by talking to God about them, seeing what His Word says, and letting spiritual friends help you "clean it out."

And you heal. With Jesus, on purpose.

That doesn't mean you have to put your entire life on hold and it's the only thing you focus on. It does mean you set aside time to handle it and give yourself grace in the other responsibilities you're managing at the same time.

It's not easy. It sucks. There was a reason you stashed them away and it was probably pain.

But with God, it's possible to confront and heal anything. Stop distracting yourself with everything else.

CHALLENGE:

Go through your life and reprioritize activities that are essential to your spiritual and emotional healing over tasks that are simply keeping you busy.

THE DANGER IN DISTRACTIONS

JEREMIAH 2:11-13

Be careful where your passion takes you.

Racism is wrong. God disagrees with it. And regardless of what anyone says or the examples we see, no one can love and follow God while actively supporting racism. Period.

That said, the dangerous thing about the powerful call for racial reconciliation and justice is that we can be tempted to put our life's hope in that instead of God.

During the string of events that followed George Floyd's death, my thoughts were consumed. I couldn't stop thinking about racial inequality, the segregated faith community in America, the racism I had personally faced, the fear of people I love becoming the next hashtag and a hundred other things. It was mentally, emotionally and physically exhausting.

I often begged God to help me see the situation spiritually because I felt like I was burning alive with anger. I didn't understand how I was supposed to reconcile what was going on with His call to love all people.

As I fought to find perspective, I recognized that there was a bigger picture. Racism is a result of evil here on Earth. And if racism went away tomorrow, it wouldn't eternally save anyone. Evil would still exist. It would just manifest in different ways.

We should always be indignant over racism and other issues that are similarly grotesque. But putting our entire hope in solving them would be misplaced. We have to be careful not to let our activism and philanthropy become our broken cistern of hope.

A cistern is an artificial reservoir for storing liquids, especially water.[5] It's meant to sustain a household or group of people. By comparing it to a spring of living water, God is making the point that Israel is using an artificial source of nourishment as a substitute for the real nurturing they were meant to find in God.

On top of that, their cisterns were broken and couldn't hold water at all. They were expecting satisfaction while looking for it from something that was incapable of giving it to them.

When we cope by placing our hope in things that are noble, worthy and important instead of God, we are still left unfulfilled, drained and disappointed regardless of the outcome.

Hoping in God doesn't mean we still can't advocate for causes close to our hearts. Passion and ambition for the greater good are essential.

But Jesus' goal was always our salvation through a loving relationship with God. So as worthy as a cause is, creating a purpose and hope outside of His context is pouring everything we have into something that won't sustain us in the long run.

We all have different callings. How can you use what you're passionate about for God and His ultimate purpose to save people? Because that's what Jesus did. Otherwise, it can become a broken cistern instead of your living water.

CHALLENGE:

Brainstorm ways you can use your passions in the context of God's eternal purpose.

IN CONTEXT OF GOD

2 CORINTHIANS 10:3-5

Nothing else works.

One day last year, I went to the store after a really hard week and was standing in the alcohol section looking for some Angry Orchards. I felt like going home to chill, drink one and watch a movie.

Except that when I considered the reason behind my desire to drink, it was because I had a hard week and not the usual because I like how cider tastes.

There's nothing wrong with drinking in moderation or watching a movie. But I was going to things that had no power beyond the moment while ignoring those that did.

So instead of buying what I came in for, I left that aisle, bought the toothpaste I needed anyway and went home to vent to God about my week. I still watched the movie afterward.

In this passage, God is trying to help us see that difference in power. The power to fix any life situation comes from using the spiritual weapons He gave us. The other things we run to might make us feel better or get us through the night, but don't have the capacity to improve anything, especially with strongholds.

A stronghold is a well-fortified place of security or survival.[6] Having a stronghold in your life means you have a sin or situation that's protected by other conditions.

For example, a relationship you want to end but have a house, a public image, joint bills, kids and dogs together. Leaving that one situation entails a lot more than just changing one thing because you've built so much of your life around it. It can be overwhelming.

That's often when we find ourselves standing in the alcohol aisle at the grocery store - or using our other negative coping methods of choice. Instead of spending the energy to go through that process step-by-step, we procrastinate, give up, numb out, or distract ourselves to make it bearable.

None of that will help.

When you're truly ready to be free from those strongholds, spiritual weapons are the only ones that work. And they don't kind of work. When you apply them to your life they will demolish, annihilate, obliterate, crush and decimate anything standing between you and freedom. It takes obedience to God, but it works.

So the next time you find yourself wanting to cope with something other than the weapons God has given you, choose power in the long run over comfort in the moment.

Check your faith. Believe that God's way works. Then instead of fighting the way the world does, use the spiritual tools we talked about in Ephesians 6:10-17. Breathe and do the next right thing.

POWER OVER COMFORT

LUKE 11:24-26

Replace your furniture.

I've moved over 35 times in my life. When I was playing in the WNBA it was twice a year. The seasons were only four months in the summer so then I'd go to Europe and play in the "off-season." I took three giant suitcases and two carry-ons for seven months in a country that many times I'd never been to before.

It was intense, but once we arrived the team always gave us our own apartment. Even though my agent, Boris, made sure I had a great apartment every time, the only thing included was basic furniture.

The first thing I always did when I got there was put my apartment together. I felt like it was really hard to invest in my new team and city if the place I was going to every day didn't feel like a home.

I put my clothes away instead of living out of a suitcase, hung up pictures and rearranged the furniture how I wanted. I went shopping for new bedding and kitchen items, whatever I needed to make my place comfortable.

Then I found my favorite grocery store and my regular place to order takeout. I tried to get all of it done within the first week so an unfamiliar place became familiar as quickly as possible.

That's what I think of when I read this passage. When we start following Jesus, we're essentially moving into a new place with just the bare necessities.

In the process, we got rid of our old behaviors that were against God's will, the friends who didn't support our new lifestyle, the inappropriate language we used and specific to this chapter, the ways we used to cope with our feelings. Our spiritual house was swept clean and put in order.

We're missing all the homey touches though. We need things that make this new life feel like ours.

Because unless we replace everything we cleaned out with spiritual alternatives, we'll make it harder for ourselves to continue living there. At some point, we may not be strong enough to continue without slipping back into our old patterns of behavior.

And just like when you cheat on a diet and it's never just one cookie, it's not going to be just one sin either. The Bible says it will be seven times worse.

So the question we have to ask ourselves is, have we replaced the things we used to cope with?

What did you replace alcohol with? What did you

replace sex with? What do replace eating with? What did you replace clubbing with? What did you replace gossip with? What did you replace selfish ambition with?

Each of those things served a purpose and fulfilled a need in your life. The only way to make this new life somewhere you actually want to stay is by finding spiritual ways to meet those same needs and deal with those same feelings. Otherwise, you'll eventually go back to your former ways of coping.

Make these decisions ahead of time because it's a lot easier than when you're in the moment fighting to survive and stay faithful.

CHALLENGE:

What are your unhealthy coping mechanisms? Find your triggers and replace your old habits with ones that help you instead.

REPLACE
WHAT YOU GOT RID OF

LET THE PAIN DO ITS WORK

HEBREWS 12:7-13

Coach got us bad with this one.

Freshman year in college, I skipped class all the time. If a class met three times a week, there was a very good chance I was going to miss one of them.

One time, I convinced my roommate and teammate, Ashley, to skip class with me for her first time ever. And of course later that day we got a call from Coach Foster, telling us to meet him in his office.

When we got there, all the seniors on our team were there too. Coach Foster told us that since the seniors obviously didn't make sure the freshman knew skipping class was wrong, we were all going to get up at six in the morning the next day and they were going to run a timed mile while we watched.

We looked at him, horrified, and then started begging. We begged him to let us run instead because we didn't want them to be punished for us. Turns out they were in on it and he was never going to make them run.

He did make us get up and run a timed mile the next morning in his effort to teach us the importance of going to class. It was his way of keeping us in school, on track to graduate and eligible to play basketball.

Once again, God is like a coach. When He causes or allows something difficult in our lives, it's to teach or train us. Sometimes it's because we've done something wrong in a specific situation and other times it's to mature us in a particular way.

Either way, when we struggle or feel pain it's not meant to discourage us. Even the worst situations can help us grow by training us to be right in God's eyes. But we have to allow the pain to serve its purpose instead of running from it by coping in a harmful way.

God is a loving Father who is trying to raise us to be righteous kids. The journey may feel unpredictable, heavy, or even impossible at times. Still, God promises that if we learn from the training the results will be worth it.

As long as the ultimate result is Heaven, the ends always justify the means.

CHALLENGE:

Don't run from the discipline by coping because it's painful. As you're fighting through it, ask yourself what God is trying to teach you in the process.

MATTHEW 11:28-30

"Ok, please help me."

As someone who spent the first 32 years of my life depending on myself, I can easily slip right back into that. It actually happened last month.

There I was, trying to figure out how to write this book, lead ministries, mentor women, love people, and fit in some semblance of self-care. I was trying to do all of it for God instead of with God.

And it was funny because God didn't take away the responsibilities. He never does.

He just continued to walk with me, whispering, "Hey, do you want to talk about all that so I can help?" And I was just walking along, sometimes not realizing, sometimes ignoring, the fact that I was carrying everything.

Eventually, I got too tired of lugging it all around and ended up in a puddle of tears in my car sobbing, "God I can't do this life!" Not even the day. The whole life. I was done!

I always picture Him saying, "About time." Then I prayed, asked for help, got a game plan from the Bible and ended up feeling a million times lighter. It's always the same outcome.

In our determination to do this life without asking for or accepting help, we get weary. But the answer to doing more without falling apart or negatively coping is to give our burdens to Jesus.

By depending on the one all-powerful God for help, we won't have to desperately run to other things for support.

God's deepest desire is to have an intimate, loving relationship with each of us. He genuinely wants to walk through every day together, listening to the things we care about, being excited, and doing anything He can to contribute.

Jesus wants to partner with you on everything you're doing for the glory of God and doesn't want to limit His plans to what you can carry alone. He dreams bigger! Taking some of the weight and pressure from you allows Him to do more through you. None of it is heavy to Him.

He's gentle, humble and faithfully there, asking to help and ready to give you rest. If what you're carrying is heavy, you're carrying too much of the load.

Jesus is like, "I got you, let's do this together."

Take an inventory of what you're trying to carry yourself. Tell God everything about each of those burdens and ask for His help.

WHAT'S HEAVY TO YOU ISN'T HEAVY TO GOD.

PHILIPPIANS 4:6-7

Sensitive content for self-harm warning.

I held my lighter underneath my desk in high school drafting class as I flicked it on and off in the back of the room. No one noticed but I wouldn't have cared if they did.

As I sat there, contemplating life, there were a million questions as to why I felt the way I did. I was popular, Mom and Daddy worked really hard to give us a great life, and by that time I could go to any college I wanted on a basketball scholarship.

So why did I feel like a fake? Why did I want to quit life half the time? Why did everyone know of me but few really knew me? Why did I feel so much pressure to be perfect?

I felt the metal on the top of the lighter get hot. Then, in a moment of impulse, I turned it over and touched it to my skin. I knew it shouldn't make me feel better but for some reason, at that moment feeling pain I could both understand and control was beautiful to me.

That was the beginning of years of self-harming behavior, the evidence of which I can still see by the scars on my hands and wrists.

We started this conversation on coping by saying that it involves specific things we do to deal with and attempt to overcome problems and difficulties. This passage of Scripture is an example of coping in a positive way that will ultimately heal us. Prayer is a big part of coping with Jesus.

Where we get into trouble with coping is when we're so determined to go through something on our terms like I was that we're willing to harm ourselves to control what we feel, how much and when.

When we have an unhealthy relationship with control it will lead to unhealthy methods of coping.

But when we surrender our control to God, trusting that going through life on His terms will be doable and beneficial to us in the long run, we'll give up our need to control situations and use healing coping strategies instead.

Prayer is how we do that and this passage is the formula. I could've put this at the end of every chapter in this book because really, it's the answer to everything. It literally says, "In every situation."

Prayer + Petition + Thanksgiving = Peace

Prayer is the overall conversation with and the eventual submission to God about what's happening, how you're feeling about it and what you want to come from it.

Petition is requesting a specific outcome and sharing with God why you think it's a good idea that He honors that request. How cool is it that God tells us to petition Him?

Thanksgiving is thanking God for who He is and what He's doing regardless of His answer.

While the formula is simple, it's not always easy and definitely takes some emotional labor to come out on the other side of it. However, the result will always be peace, even in situations that are beyond your understanding.

I'm personally thankful for this formula. Now when a self-harming thought pops into my head it's a signal to pray instead of going to find a lighter, alcohol, or any of the other things I used to regularly cope with. It's definitely given me a positive way to consistently cope with challenging situations and feelings.

So whenever you're feeling troubled about any-thing, follow this Scripture and watch God's peace replace your anxious feelings.

CHALLENGE:

When you're tempted to cope, ask yourself, is this behavior healing or harming?
Then apply this formula. Practice until prayer is your first option.

PRAYER IS OXYGEN   PRAYER IS OXYGEN   PRAYER IS OXYGEN

PRAYER IS OXYGEN   PRAYER IS OXYGEN   PRAYER IS OXYGEN

PRAYER IS OXYGEN   PRAYER IS OXYGEN   PRAYER IS OXYGEN

8. RES

ToRED

(A Conversation About Restoration)

THE LIFE OF ABUSE, WELFARE, AND ROACHES WAS REPLACED WITH ONE OF FAMILY DINNERS, VACATION BIBLE SCHOOL, AND SPORTS

I always say Daddy saved the life I have by rescuing me from what could have been.

As you recall, after my parents got divorced my sisters and I went to live with Mommy, despite her mental illness. At that point, Daddy didn't have much understanding of what her condition entailed and I'm positive she didn't realize the severity of it either.

What followed was three years of neglect and abuse. It wasn't her fault. At all. She wasn't well enough to take care of us and looking back, the system failed her too.

Even though in third grade I knew something was wrong, I didn't know what to do about it. Part of me wanted to tell Daddy and the other part wanted to protect Mommy. I wanted us to be okay but I wanted her to be okay too.

For two years, there didn't seem to be a good solution so I didn't do anything outside of learning to survive.

Until one day, me glancing across the room at her escalated into the worst physical fight we'd had. I ended up hiding in my room once again, wedged up against the door to make sure she couldn't open it. I waited there.

Once I heard her bedroom door close and knew she had gone into her room, I made a break for it.

On the way out I quickly searched our small apartment. I found Kristin curled up on the kitchen floor, crying between the dishwasher and the wall, grabbed her hand and pulled her out the front door behind me.

We ran across our apartment complex to our babysitters, Edith and Robert's, house. Edith listened to what happened and then got up to call our Grandma. While she was on the phone I sprawled across the living room carpet and wrote a letter to Daddy.

It began, "Dear Daddy, don't be scared, but you have to come get us." I paused, trying to decide what should come next. Although I felt guilty for telling on Mommy, I knew things would continue to get worse if I didn't do something.

So I kept writing: "I didn't want to tell you, but Mommy is hitting us and doing other mean things. We can't stand it anymore. I want to come live with you and Kristin does too. And I'm sure Amber wouldn't mind. Please come soon. I love you."

I closed the finished card and couldn't help but smile at the cover. It had a little bear on the front crying into her hands over an empty honey pot, saying, "I can't bear it anymore." It felt appropriate.

It turned out that Edith called Daddy long before he got my card. Once he found out what was going on, he started the process of getting custody of us.

A couple months later we went to live with Daddy and his new wife, Nylene (who we called Mom). The life of abuse, welfare and roaches was replaced with one of family dinners, Vacation Bible School and sports. It wasn't all rainbows but they tried to give us the best life they could.

That's one thing I love about God too. When He comes to get us and we decide to live with Him, restoration always comes afterward.

Restoring something means to return it back to how it originally was[7] - I always think of how beautiful older restored cars are. God doesn't want to leave us in the same condition He found us, in the same situations that damaged us. His plan is always to restore, heal, and make us like new.

That means getting back to the trusting, obedient, blessed relationship that Adam and Eve had with God in the Garden of Eden. For us it would be how we might have looked at God with innocence and wonder if we learned about Him as kids, assuming His goodness before life made us question it.

God wants to bring us back to that. He did His part by sending Jesus and continues it by showing us we're loved every day. Now it's up to us to decide how we're going to respond.

Let's study it out.

A STUDY ON RESTORATION

Please read each Scripture before you read each devotional.
God's words are more important than mine.

ACTS 22:2-16

I just waht to be right(eous).

The first spiritual mentor I had was amazing. Her name was Lynn, and no one would've thought she'd be my mentor. She was quiet, reserved and you might even call her timid. But she was brilliant and also loved God with all her heart.

One day, we were doing a Bible study and she confronted me about my pride in prioritizing my feelings over what the Bible said.

When she first pointed it out to me, I didn't agree at all. She wasn't the type to argue so she told me to go home, look over the Scriptures we talked about and let her know what I thought.

When I got home, I started to look up Scriptures so that I could call her the next day and prove her wrong. I was really doing a whole other Bible study with myself at eleven o'clock at night.

Then it popped into my head to pray.

I said, "God, I know I'm right. So please help me show her. But, I want to please You more than I want to be right so if I'm wrong, show me."

I said amen and then went to sleep, determined to pick up my quest for truth again in the morning.

When I woke up, I opened the Bible to one of the Scriptures we read the night before and there was exactly what Lynn had said, staring me right in the face.

It was so clear to the point where I said out loud, "Wow. How did I get this wrong?"

I called her immediately, apologized, and asked her to show me how I could be better for God. I was so thankful that God had opened my spiritual eyes and used Lynn to do it.

Paul was sure he was right too. But he wasn't.

In many of the passages about healing in the Bible, the people who needed to be healed called out to Jesus because they knew they needed help. Not Paul. He didn't see his need. So God took his physical sight to show him his spiritual blindness.

We won't go to God to be healed if we don't see our need for healing. So He causes or allows things to happen to get our attention. The goal is to make us question what we think we already know.

It can be as benign as a conversation with someone who cares about us or as extreme as allowing a physical sickness to illustrate a spiritual one.

However God chooses to solicit our attention, our hearts have to be soft to the fact that our eyes might need to be opened, even if we think we can already see. We have to want to be right with God more than we want to be right.

Are you willing to question what you already know about God in order to see your deeper need for Him? Are you willing to be wrong in order to be made righteous?

CHALLENGE:

Even when you believe you're right, acknowledge the fact that there might be more to see. Then like Paul, be humble enough to allow someone to help you see deeper.

THE BLIND WILL SEE

JOHN 5:1-9

My body decided it was done playing basketball before I did.

I had three potentially career-ending injuries, back-to-back-to-back. First I broke my knee cap, then I tore my Achilles tendon, then I tore my ACL (Anterior Cruciate Ligament). It was crushing.

After I tore my ACL I told my agent, Boris, that I was going to retire. I was tired of the heartbreak and the grind of trying to come back. Most of all, I was tired of hoping that the next time was going to be different.

He asked me if I still wanted to play. Of course I wanted to but coming back would take a lot and I didn't know if I could do all of that.

Boris said teams still wanted me and asked me to think about it for a few days before he told them I wasn't interested. My gut reaction was to say no, but I agreed to give it some time.

Over the next three days I thought about trying again. And I counted all the costs I would have to pay to come back:

The nine months of intense physical therapy, treatment, and workouts that would go into taking my body from not being able to walk to competing against the top 1% in the world.

The aches, pains and sore muscles that accompanied that process.

The physical, mental and emotional energy it would take to hope this injury was the last injury and that the work would finally be worth it.

As I thought through all I had done and would have to do, I tried to decide if the effort would be worth it and if I had the hope to do it.

Three days later I called Boris and told him I was in. I was going to try one more time.

When I picture the man at the well trying to answer Jesus' questions, this is how I see him.

Jesus' question of, "Do you want to get well," seems like it had an obvious answer. Of course the man wanted to get well. Yet what Jesus was really asking was, "Are you willing to try again?"

Jesus knew He could heal the man. What He needed to know was if, after countless times hoping for a miracle in the 38 years he'd been unable to walk, the man was willing to try, differently this time.

The man's first response was one of hopelessness. He had no reason to believe healing was possible because he had been disappointed so many times. I picture him thinking back to each one of those disappointments while looking at the pool he couldn't get into. Surely there was no way he could be healed.

But Jesus didn't worry about what had happened before. He knew there was another way. So He told him what to do. And as the man did it, he was healed.

We can get caught up in hopelessness, thinking restoration is impossible because of all the ways we've tried before that didn't work. But with Jesus, it's never a matter of ability. We can absolutely do it. It's always a question of willingness.

Jesus is ready and waiting to heal you, your situation, and your entire life if needed. But it's not up to Him. It's up to you. Do you want to get well? And are you willing to try again, His way this time?

CHALLENGE:

Count the cost. Decide that you're going to try again. Commit to giving up your way to try Jesus' way.

LOOK FORWARD

HE'S WAITING FOR YOU
HE'S WAITING FOR YOU
HE'S WAITING FOR YOU
HE'S WAITING FOR YOU
HE'S WAITING FOR YOU
HE'S WAITING FOR YOU
HE'S WAITING FOR YOU
HE'S WAITING FOR YOU
HE'S WAITING FOR YOU
HE'S WAITING FOR YOU
HE'S WAITING FOR YOU
HE'S WAITING FOR YOU

LUKE 15:11-24

I walked away on purpose and He took me back.

There was a time when I was really trying to find God. I had started reading my Bible, was going to church and stopped doing all of the things I knew I wasn't supposed to do. At that time I didn't know if I was doing it right according to the Bible, but I was genuinely trying.

Then, it happened. You know that one person who has always been your weakness? I swear we all have one.

Well that one for me came back and for the first time wanted to be with me and me only. I had to decide between God and that relationship. To my shame, I chose the relationship.

After God had fought for me, proven Himself to me and improved my life in so many ways, I knowingly chose to turn my back on Him and go back to my old life. For six months I was caught in the same sins God had fought to free me of.

When that relationship ended, I was broken, even to the point of being suicidal. I knew I could go back to God - He had proven it to me a million times - but I was so ashamed that I had hurt Him by leaving.

So I waited as long as I could. And when nothing else helped, I went back.

I am the prodigal son in so many ways. There's no reason God should've taken me back or given me anything more. He did it simply because it's who He is. His love endures forever, remember?

We've all fallen and failed God. Restoration comes after we come back to Him, not before. Don't try to clean yourself up before you come. Just come.

In any area you've turned your back on Him, come.

God will run to meet you, change your clothes and restore your position. But you have to come back.

CHALLENGE:

Let go of anything that is keeping you from running into God's arms. He's waiting to run to meet you.

DEUTERONOMY 9:20-21

Repentance - a change of heart that leads to a change in action

The biggest idol that I put before God was impurity in relationships. As I shared with you, it even pulled me off my path to finding God a couple times before actually committing to Him. I had to learn to put God above my relationships.

Now in living a life of purity for Him, I work to make it easier on myself to stay that way, and make sure God feels loved in the process.

I often look at Him as an actual person so I can figure out what I can do to help Him feel more loved. I think that's part of the reason God created us in His image, so we could draw the parallels between our desires and His.

As far as purity goes, I know that if someone I was with was constantly flirting with his ex's, it would be hard for me to feel loved and secure in that relationship. I never want to make God feel that way so I'm intentional about not doing things that might.

I stopped listening to music with heavy sexual content. If a scene in a movie goes beyond kissing, I fast forward so I don't see it. On my social media there are a lot of beautiful people that I love but don't follow - or at least mute their posts - because they show a lot of their bodies in their pictures.

I keep my life very safe in the area of purity to maintain and show my loyalty to God.

So the first time I read this passage it struck me as the most complete example of what repentance is supposed to look like in our lives. But also, what it would look like if I was trying my hardest to help God feel loved and secure after I cheated on Him.

When Moses saw that the people of Israel had made an idol out of a golden calf to worship instead of God, he was furious. To save Israel from God's anger, he didn't just get rid of the idol.

He burned it, crushed it, ground it into dust, and then threw the dust into a stream that was going down a mountain. He did everything possible to make sure it was completely out of their lives.

If we want to come back to God after cheating on Him, this is what our heart should be.

As we're trying to live differently, we need to get rid of whatever is going to make that harder. A lot of times we want to keep one foot in, one foot out and bet on our newfound resolve. But if we were strong enough to resist, we'd have done it already.

If you're reading this and there's something you're wondering if you should get rid of, the answer is probably yes.

I know it's hard. That's why we talked about counting the cost and being willing to do what it takes. You don't have to get rid of everything in your life. Just anything that makes it easier to cheat on God.

As you grow in Jesus, the things you need to give up may evolve. But commit 100% of your focus to staying faithful to God and making sure He feels your love. That means treating your temptations like Moses treated Israel's golden calf.

CHALLENGE:

Survey your life. Completely and totally get rid of anything that's going to make it harder for you to follow God in the areas you're struggling with.

EXTREME REPENTANCE

HOSEA 10:12, EZEKIEL 36:24-28

Those roots of hurt ran deep.

I used to be that girl who cared too much, cried too much and wore her emotions on her sleeve. Then I had one too many "I'll never feel like this again" moments. I learned it wasn't safe to be that girl and so I got off the rollercoaster of feelings by choosing not to feel.

I stopped letting people get close enough to hurt me, started pretending it was possible not to care, and treated people as disposable before they could treat me that way. Even when I became a Christian, that was still my heart towards people in a lot of ways.

Until God showed me.

My spiritual mentor, Jalisa, and I were talking about how I wanted to help women find God. Very gently, she looked at me and said, "Chantelle, you will never be able to help the kind of women you want to help without vulnerability and love, because they have everything else."

Her statement hit me like a brick in the face.

The thing I wanted to do most in life was help women like me fall in love with Jesus. But life had taught me that love and vulnerability were dangerous. What she said meant accepting the risk that someone would shatter the feelings I didn't want to have in the first place. I was deflated by the realization that she was right.

As God tried to convince me to soften my heart again just like this passage says, I fought Him every step of the way. Until He reminded me, "Chantelle, you crucified Jesus and He lets you close every day. He loves you anyway." There was nothing I could do to argue with that.

So I chose to start breaking up the unplowed ground of my hard heart. As I did my part to obey, read, pray, forgive and redefine what I thought relationships were supposed to look like, God did His part in softening my heart.

In the process, I was reminded what it felt like to be hurt by someone you give your heart to. It was painful and I hated it. Still, God showed me that He was there to comfort me, protect me in my pain, and return the love I gave to others.

Part of restoration is building enough trust in God's love and protection that you allow your heart to be soft again. You allow yourself to feel and take your feelings to God.

Because the answer to healing isn't surviving with a hard heart. It's living with a soft heart and a powerful Father.

Choose to trust people enough to be vulnerable in small ways. As they prove you right you'll grow closer and be able to open up more. As they prove you wrong, you'll learn discernment and dependence on God.

A SOFT HEART AND A POWERFUL FATHER

really didn't like men.

I was sitting in a meeting with another spiritual mentor, Elizabeth, when she looked at me thoughtfully and said, "You don't like men, you just tolerate them." My spiritual mentors be coming for my life!

My mouth fell open before I very quickly and automatically denied it. She said, "No, look around at the men in your life. You don't like them. You tolerate them."

When I actually thought about it, she was right. Somewhere along the way I had stopped seeing men as actual people with feelings.

As I dug deeper, part of the reason was that I still had residual feelings from my sexual assault. And part of it was from living in a culture of men acting callously towards women. Regardless of why I saw men like that, I knew it wasn't okay and that I had to change it.

The pattern of relationships in this world is to be selective with our love based on our preferences, trauma, other people's behavior, or our feelings. I had fallen right into that. But when God tells us to love each other He's talking about all people, not just women or just men or just anyone else.

The only way to train ourselves to do something new is to force ourselves to do it until it becomes a natural part of who we are. That's what God means by making our lives living sacrifices. We have to be willing to sacrifice what we want for what God says until our mind is transformed to the point that they're the same thing.

In biblical times, when animals were sacrificed they were killed on an altar. Now God tells us to be a living sacrifice, which means sometimes, we're going to want to squirm off the altar to avoid the pain of dying to our mindsets and desires.

That's why gratitude is so important. When we don't want to do whatever God says, it's our thankfulness for His mercy in Jesus' sacrifice that should motivate us to do it anyway. Jesus chose to stay on the Cross when He could've gotten off.

Even though what Elizabeth said was hard to hear, I'm glad she said it. Without her insight I wouldn't have so many amazing, loving, spiritual men in my life now. They would've been here, but I wouldn't have been open to seeing who they were.

As you continue to walk this path with God, be open to retraining any thoughts that match the pattern of the world to match the pattern of the Bible instead. It will restore your mind to where God wants it to be. That's when you'll be able to see God's plan for your life more clearly.

As you find patterns in your life that are from the world and not God's Word, commit to changing them, even if it feels like staying on the altar when you want to jump off.

TRANSFORMATION FOLLOWS SACRIFICE

LUKE 23:26-34

Forgiveness is for you.

The most difficult person for me to forgive was Mommy. I blamed her for a lot of hard things in my life.

Until I took a graduate-level class on mental illness during my senior year of college. We went to a work program one day to interview some of its members about their lives and experiences. I was shocked by how much the woman I was talking to reminded me of Mommy. They didn't look similar, but their behavior was almost exact.

One of the questions we were supposed to ask was, "What was your diagnosis?" And when she answered, it was the same illness Mommy had. It helped me realize how much of Mommy's behavior had been because of her illness and not because of her as a person.

Mommy had been a prominent physical therapist, married to her college sweetheart, living in Southern California with three kids and close to her family. Mental illness stole her dream life from her. And while she did have her own choices that she made, for the first time I saw her as a hurting person instead of a bad one.

I forgave her on the spot and it felt like a 100-pound weight I didn't know I was carrying disappeared.

That's how Jesus saw the people crucifying Him. Although it hurt Him, He knew that what they were doing was because they were broken by sin and that they didn't understand. He also knew only a relationship with God could save them, which is why He came.

Jesus took nothing personally. And so deciding to forgive people is deciding to have the heart of Jesus.

Forgiveness doesn't make the things that were done to us acceptable. They were still wrong. It does acknowledge that we're all damaged in different ways and we all need God. That includes you, and the people who hurt you.

Forgiveness also recognizes that nothing anyone else has been done to us is worse than what we did to Jesus. Our sins killed an innocent man who was also God.

As we try to live this life for God, connecting with that is the only practice that will keep us from being self-righteous and judgemental towards others.

And so if we're going to ask God to forgive us for killing His Son, we have to be willing to do the same for others in their wrongs against us.

Sometimes though, the hardest person to forgive is yourself.

I had to forgive myself for the shame I walked in for too long, the people I hurt, the stupid things I did to feel worthy when God said I was chosen all along and so many other things.

It's a battle but it's worth fighting for it.

Forgive yourself for the relationships you stayed in that weren't loving.

Forgive yourself for the shame you stayed in as a result of other people's actions.

Forgive yourself for hurting people when you were hurting.

Forgive yourself for not being able to fix someone else.

Own whatever you did and forgive yourself for all of it. Then forgive others. Not because they deserve it. But because neither do you and Jesus asked God to forgive you anyway.

CHALLENGE:

Pray. Then write a letter of forgiveness to yourself in a tone that would be safe for a crying child. Next, write a letter to the other people you need to forgive. You don't have to give it to them. Just write it.

FORGIVE BROKEN PEOPLE WE'RE ALL BROKEN PEOPLE

ONE

TRUTH. LORD. SAVIOR.

JOHN 14:6-7

This devotional is completely counter-cultural.

For a long time, I looked for someone to save me from myself, my insecurity, my loneliness and my sadness. I was waiting for someone to come and sweep me off my feet. And I've been in relationships with some amazing people who, in doing their best, have shown me how I deserved to be treated.

Still, as wonderful as they were, none of them could save me. Because at the end of the day they were people too, with their own struggles, who needed saving just like I did.

Throughout life, I've found that I'm not the only one who has had to learn this. I've had so many conversations with women who put all their hope into a person - usually a man - to save them.

I somewhat blame Disney for selling us this narrative that every princess needs to be saved. And it is partly true. We all do need saving. But here's the rest of it. There is only one Prince who can save us and He already came.

No one else has the power to save you. Not a husband. Not a wife. Not a president. Not crystals. Not self-help books. Not social change. Not chakras.

Not Budda - he's dead. Not Muhammad - he's dead. Not Mary - she's dead.

Not anyone but Jesus.

Culturally we've been told to accept a "choose your own spirituality" path to Heaven. So I understand that my saying this might make some people uncomfortable and offend others. But Jesus said it first.

We were separated from God by our sins and because of His overwhelming love, Jesus came to repair and restore that relationship. No one else did. In a restored relationship with God, we get love, peace, joy, confidence, comfort, purpose, freedom and salvation. Only through Jesus.

This is important because if you want your life restored, you can't flirt with different belief systems and try different ways. You can't look for people to save you like I did. You can't blame hypocritical Christians for misrepresenting Him, even though you wouldn't be wrong.

The fact is that there's one path to God and He's it. Restoration doesn't exist without Jesus.

CHALLENGE:

Fight the temptation to look for another savior by reading the Bible every day so you can fall more in love with the One who already came to save you.

MARK 10:24-31

I've learned incredible lessons in the last 7 years with God.

I learned how to cultivate intimate relationships without physical intimacy. It's ironic how pure relationships are so much smoother.

I learned that the cure for my worry was letting go of my need to control everything and trusting God instead.

I learned how to do life with people without competing or constantly protecting myself, and to heal from the trauma that made me feel like I had to.

I learned that when I put God's purpose first He blesses everything else I do. And that it always comes with joy.

I learned that in the hardest times God always shows up with peace, comfort and love. And that His presence is tangible.

I could go on and on and on about what I've learned since choosing to follow the Bible and I'm thankful for all of the lessons. I absolutely love my life.

Most of all, I'm thankful for God, my Father, and my Lord; for pursuing me, courting me, waiting for me, saving me, and walking with me daily.

I did have to give up a lot for this life. But the life I have now is worth so much more than I gave up in unquestionably every way.

That's what Jesus promised His disciples in this passage. A rich man had just walked away from a chance to follow Jesus. He had a lot going for him, but he loved his money more than he loved God.

Jesus' disciples had given up everything themselves to follow Him. So when they saw this they needed a little reassurance that they had made the right choice.

We all have that "one thing" that's the hardest to give up when choosing to follow God. For me, as I shared, it was control over my relationships. Sometimes we can look around at what other people have and question our decision.

But Jesus makes us a promise that everything we give up to follow Him will be worth it - not easy, but worth it - both in this life and in eternity.

Anything worth having is going to cost you something. Jesus isn't pretending that eternity is free. It costs your life. He does promise, however, that it'll be worth whatever you have to pay for it.

Commit to prioritizing Jesus over everything, even your "one thing."

THE COST WILL ALWAYS BE WORTH IT

GALATIANS 6:7-9

Sow what you want to see.

After I retired from playing basketball and left coaching, I spent almost four years in medical device sales. It was capital sales so it had an incredibly long sales cycle, meaning I could start working on a project and the sale probably wouldn't close until six to eighteen months later.

When my manager, Austin, first handed me a brand new sales territory, he told me, "Don't worry about selling anything for the first six months. Just go to your accounts and start making friends."

So that's what I did. I focused on building relationships for the first six months and barely sold anything. A year in, I was still doing all the work behind the scenes and while it started to pick up, I still wasn't selling a lot.

Sometimes it was hard to persevere without seeing the numbers I wanted. There were late nights and early mornings. But I kept telling myself that all my hard work would eventually pay off.

And it did. Fifteen months after I started, I closed a $2.9 million deal that covered four hospitals. That year overall, I sold $3.2 million worth of medical equipment. Because I showed up every day and did the work.

That's what God is telling us in this passage. We will get out whatever we consistently put in. There is no cheating the process and there's no cheating God.

Depending on how we look at this, it can be taken as a promise or a warning.

If we're consistently working hard, putting in extra time, or filling our lives with godly things, it's eventually going to show. If we're slacking, taking shortcuts, or filling our lives with foolishness, that's going to show too.

Fruits mirror seeds, outputs mirror inputs, and we can always tell what we planted by what we harvested in every area of life.

We play a major role in our own restoration.

So as you're making hard decisions to stay on the altar, make changes, and transform your mind, trust that God will bless your perseverance.

Don't get discouraged if the results don't come right away. It often gets harder before it gets easier. But trust that as you keep sowing into the future life you want with God, you will eventually reap the fruit you've been planting. It's both a principle of life and a promise of God.

Persevere in continuing to plant the seeds of the fruit you want to eat. Make changes in any area that you don't like what you're growing.

PERSEVERANCE PAYS OFF

9. F

REE

(A Conversation About Freedom)

IT'S ABOUT LEARNING HOW TO RIDE THE WIND

A couple of years ago, I came across a song by Beautiful Eulogy called, "The String That Ties Us." It was originally based on an old parable about a kite. I was so inspired by it that I made a kite the icon of my Confidently His brand. My adapted version of the story goes like this:

The quest for freedom is literally in a kite's design. They were created to fly. So let's say a kite grew a consciousness and became like a person.

First thought: Wheeeeeeeeee, I'm flying!!! Second thought: What the heck is this string and why is it holding me back?!

So of course, in a moment of courage and rebellion, the kite cuts the string. It goes soaring off into the sky, flying with the ups and downs of the wind, tasting "true" freedom for the first time.

Until things take a turn for the worst.

The kite, not being anchored by the string and steady hand of its owner, begins a nosedive. Just as quickly as she soared into the sky, she ends up on the ground in a pile of broken pieces.

It was a pain she had never felt before. And in that moment the kite realized that even though she felt like the string was holding her back, it was really protecting her, enabling her to fly in the first place.

The kite is me, you and our friends. The string is the Bible and the owner is God. We were created to fly, yet there will always be situations when we feel restrained by the Bible and held back by God.

And sometimes we have to end up broken to realize or admit that no matter how amazing we were designed to be, we can only truly fly and experience freedom in the hands of the One who made us.

In our lives we have a choice. To either be held back by the string or held back by our brokenness that came from cutting it. Whatever comes next will be a result of the patterns we live by.

Once we've chosen to stay connected to God, from there it's just about learning how to ride the wind.

This chapter is about helping us embrace being a kite because the Bible has a lot to say about freedom.

Let's study it out.

DEAR GOD,

MAY I NEVER TRADE LASTING WHOLENESS

FOR TEMPORARY FREEDOM.

AMEN

A STUDY ON FREEDOM

Please read each Scripture before you read each devotional.
God's words are more important than mine.

ROMANS 6:16-23

It's your choice.

I used to think freedom was doing whatever I wanted. And I did that. Until what I wanted to do changed and I couldn't easily change my actions to match.

For example, when I wanted to stop cussing but said the wrong thing at the wrong time, again. Or when I wanted to stop drinking but one drink turned into five, again. Or when I wanted to stop playing with people's emotions but found myself hurting someone I cared about, again.

That's when I realized two things: One, I wasn't free. And two, the freedom I wanted doesn't exist until Heaven.

Here's why.

Before I was following God, I was free to get drunk, to go out and to take home anyone I wanted.

But I was not free from feeling like crap the next morning, or the embarrassment of the drunk texts I sent. I was not free from the pregnancy scares, the need to get regular STD tests to be "safe," or the anxiousness of the waiting period.

I was not free from the drama that comes with hooking up with someone "no strings attached." I was not free from feeling emotionally connected to someone who was only physically available, or the guilt of hurting that person when I was the one not into them afterward.

Most of the time, I didn't feel free.

Now as a Christian, I'm not free to get drunk, party at clubs, or take home anyone who catches my eye. But I am free from the consequences that came with those "freedoms."

And that's just an example from one night. We don't have time to detail the rest of life.

That's exactly what this passage is telling us. The freedom many of us want doesn't exist until Heaven. So I guess what we could actually say is, "choose your chains."

Keeping it all the way real with you, this life following God can feel like slavery sometimes. Most days I absolutely love it. There are those other days though.

In some ways, I look at this relationship with God like one with anyone else. Just because you're exclusive, doesn't mean you're blind. It doesn't mean you'll never notice someone else you want, even if it's just a physical attraction and only for a second.

What being in that relationship means is that you've decided you'd rather be with the person you chose instead of whoever else you could go get. And it's the same with God.

God doesn't say you won't want what He says no to. You will feel your chains sometimes. He just says, choose me instead.

Because the freedoms He gives are better than the freedoms you'll get if you go somewhere else.

CHALLENGE:

Choose the chains of righteousness over the chains of sin.

TREAT GOD AS GOD TREAT GOD AS GOD

ROMANS 1:21-25

Check your patterns.

Home games in the WNBA were fun because I knew someone on almost every opposing team and we usually went out after. On a certain night, we started with dinner and finished at a club drinking Vodka Cranberry until it closed.

Afterward, I went home with a mutual friend of my teammate and ended up in a completely drunken one-night stand. I rushed home at five in the morning with barely enough time to shower and pack for the bus to the airport at six.

I couldn't have slept anyway. Sitting at the airport waiting for our flight, I was disgusted. In the shower I had scrubbed as hard as I could, trying to get the night off me. I could still feel it. Not in the way you crave the one you love after being intimate. More like I felt the dirtiness on my body and wanted to peel my skin off.

I was so angry at myself. This wasn't the first time I had hooked up with someone I didn't care about. After each time I would say I'd never do it again, only to find myself right back there. It was starting to become a pattern.

I had no idea why I couldn't change and unfortunately going to God for the answer didn't happen until a few years later. If I had read these Scriptures, I would've seen that it was because I wasn't treating God as God.

When we want to worship other things, God gives us the freedom to do it. As we continue repeating it, it eventually becomes who we are.

We think we're in control until we want to start making different choices and can't. When the desire is there without the power to stop making the same mistakes, we've become a slave to our character.

Thankfully, God doesn't confine us to the agonizing places our character takes us. He will allow us to go there, giving us over to it. But He doesn't banish us there forever.

Just like this exact passage would've saved me years of struggling with the same issues, when you search in the Word, it'll show you the "why" behind whatever you're struggling with.

It'll give you the power to change but in order to overcome something, you have to first see it as a problem.

CHALLENGE:

Admit that the destructive patterns in your life run deeper than being your personal choices and start giving God authority in that area.

GALATIANS 1:10

You can't please everyone.

The recruiting process for college sports is extremely intense. High profile kids have hundreds of college coaches vying for their commitment to play for them.

So when I was being recruited, while I was grateful for the opportunities, it was also overwhelming. I felt terrible knowing that I could only choose one school and that I'd have to disappoint all of the other ones. That meant saying no to some amazing options.

I ended up on the other side of that dynamic when I retired from playing basketball and became a coach at Virginia Tech University.

My strategy in recruiting was what worked for Vanderbilt in signing me. I didn't worry about how many schools the recruits were talking to because when that kid made their choice, a lot of people were going to be disappointed no matter what.

I just worked to build our relationship into one with so much value that I wasn't the person they were willing to disappoint.

Life is like a recruiting process. When it comes to pleasing people or pleasing God, most of the time someone is going to be left disappointed. We can't do both consistently so we have to pick one to commit to.

Our feelings make choosing harder. When we don't pick people, we can be made fun of, gossiped about or rejected by those disappointed in our choice.

Many times it's by the people we most want to be accepted by like our family and friends. It's heartbreaking. Sometimes we can give in just to avoid the feeling.

That chains us to an identity that varies depending on who we're around and how they feel. We'll never know who we truly are, which means losing ourselves for someone else is a guarantee.

In contrast, God is constant. When we lose ourselves in Him, we find who we were created to be. And finding your authentic self is worth losing anyone who wants you to be someone else.

Your ability to choose God over people comes from building your relationship to the point that He's the One you're not willing to disappoint, no matter how many other people you have to.

That doesn't mean you'll be excited about being

rejected or the internal conflict that can come with it. It does mean that you'll have chosen the relationship that's most valuable to you in the long run.

Then you'll be free to serve God, find yourself, and cut the chains to people's opinions.

CHALLENGE:

Be more intentional about building your relationship with God
than you are with any other person in your life.

FIRST, PLEASE GOD.

FREEDOM AND GLORY

ROMANS 8:18–21

I'm super competitive.

We were in practice one day and as usual, I was playing with the starting team. Then without warning Coach Foster moved me to the team with the players who barely played.

I looked at him like, "What the heck?" as we repeatedly got scored on. He just shrugged.

First, I was annoyed. Then I got mad. I felt like he was trying to make me lose and I didn't understand why. But I decided I was going to win anyway. I pulled the team together, made a plan, started being more vocal and worked harder. The whole time Coach stood there, smirking on the sideline.

After we won I looked at him like, "Now what," with a whole attitude. And he kept smiling.

When practice ended, he called me over and asked me what I thought his point was. Still frustrated I said, "I don't know why you wanted me to lose."

He gently and matter-of-factly said, "I didn't want you to lose. I wanted you to lead. We need you to be more of a leader and I knew you wouldn't do it unless I made you."

I looked down, embarrassed that in my frustration I hadn't trusted him. Of course Coach had a bigger purpose for what he was doing. He always did.

As does God. Everything we go through is part of His plan to set us free from anything standing between us and complete freedom. Both in this life and in eternity.

It won't always be fun and will include suffering. But in your frustration, your job is to do the same thing Coach wanted me to do: respond.

Respond by releasing whatever is holding you back. Respond by letting the frustration push you towards God instead of getting mad at Him. Respond by stepping into the person He's trying to make you through the struggle.

Just like Coach was watching me hoping I would lead, God is watching you, hoping you will choose freedom in Him instead of the comfort of staying the same.

CHALLENGE:

Trust God that His goal in whatever you're going through is freedom.

GENESIS 32:22-32

My second year serving in the ministry was rough.

It felt like no matter what I said or did it was wrong. Especially when it came to compassion and self-control.

I particularly remember this one time. I had a conversation with someone about being accountable for her actions and she started crying right in the middle of it. There I was, stuck, trying to feel compassion I hadn't cultivated when all I wanted to do was tell her to get out of her feelings.

Another time, I sat there with someone else while being disrespected and literally bit my tongue so I didn't verbally attack her in response. It only worked for so long and I ended up saying things I shouldn't have.

Every time something would trigger me in those two areas I'd respond the wrong way. It felt like I kept failing the same test over and over.

I complained to God that things weren't fair, that I was right, and that I felt like I was being held to a higher standard than other Christians when we all had the same Bible. I was tempted to think I wasn't cut out for the ministry and quit trying.

What I eventually realized was that God was wrestling with me in those areas so I could be free from them.

He was trying to replace my harshness, lack of love and carelessness with traits that glorified Him instead. Once I gave in to His plan to change me, I was able to overcome and start passing those tests instead of failing them. I've definitely seen results of empathy and composure.

This story is an example of one of the many things I love about the Old Testament in that it gives us physical demonstrations of spiritual lessons.

From previous Scriptures, Jacob had a reputation as a liar and manipulator. God had taken him on a journey to change those character flaws but in order to become who God needed him to be, there was a change that could only happen through wrestling.

So God had Jacob wrestle physically to bring about a transformation spiritually.

For us, there are changes God wants to make in our lives that can only happen through us wrestling for our character and convictions.

We can get resentful like, "God, this is hard! What the heck?" We can be tempted to give up, let go and walk away. But holding onto God and spiritually wrestling to be free is the only way we'll be blessed in the end.

Wrestle with the things you believe. Wrestle with what God is telling you to give up, or who you were in the past. Wrestle with your impure desires, your identity, your mistakes and failures.

Freedom is about perseverance. Holding onto God through pain, anger, brokenness, time, questions and doubts. Sometimes you have to wrestle yourself free.

CHALLENGE:

Refuse to let go of God through the challenges until you find the blessing on the other side.

DON'T
LET
GO

LAMENTATIONS 2:14, PROVERBS 27:6

If you love me, you'll call me out.

When I first started trying to follow God, I changed a lot about my life. Then after about a year, I met a guy that I really liked and we all but moved in together. It caused inconsistencies in my walk - to say the least - that quickly showed in my online life. One day I'd post a Bible verse and the next I'd post a song lyric about sex.

After one particularly spicy lyric, an acquaintance messaged me about the contradiction between the two. He encouraged me to be careful about sending mixed messages and not living out my faith completely.

At that point, I replied with something flippant like, "God's not done with me yet." That was my excuse not to change. But as I grew in my faith and realized that relationship had me in spiritual jail, I never forgot that he had the guts to warn me when he saw something that wasn't right.

On the other hand, during that same time I was going to a church every Sunday and prayer at six in the morning twice a week. Everyone was friendly but no one was a part of my life. No one asked about my daily spiritual walk. No one called me out on my sin, even privately. They smiled at me every week, accepted my tithes and kept it moving.

I wasn't having any hard conversations with them either though. I didn't know I was supposed to be. Culturally, we've gotten away from telling people hard truths because that love is often reclassified as judgment. Especially in many faith communities.

But here's the thing: people who don't hold you accountable don't protect you.

We do have a responsibility to read the Scriptures ourselves and obey God. But as perilous as this journey is, we'll never survive without truthful people in our corner helping us stay out of emotional, mental and spiritual captivity.

Real friends tell hard truths.

And the easier you make it for people to tell you the truth, the more truth you'll hear. Keep your heart open and humble as you listen.

We also need to be those kinds of friends. Don't let your fear of what someone will think or say get in the way of you trying to set them free. My friend did his job by telling me the truth in the most gentle, loving way he could have. How I responded was on me.

Not all correction is judgment, especially if it's done with the Bible. We were meant to help and protect each other from spiritual slavery.

Not just protect feelings, but protect actual people.

Keep people around you who will tell you the truth of the Scriptures,
even when it's something hard to say and hard to hear.

TRUST THE HARD TRUTH

JEREMIAH 29:11-14, 31:8-9

Don't drop his hand.

I was sitting in my prayer closet the other day, listening to a song by Lecrae and Tori Kelly called, "I'll Find You." It's about God coming to find us in whatever hard situation we're in.

As I was listening to the words of the song, I started crying. It caught me totally off guard. I wasn't crying because I was sad, I was crying because I was grateful.

I never would have pictured my life like it is right now, full of purpose and joy everyday. When I see pictures of me from before I started following God, I look at my eyes and remember where I was inside. And I'm like, "Wow, that girl really had no idea what God had for her."

So when I heard that song it just hit me. God came to find me. I was in the middle of a mental, emotional, and spiritual desert when He came to rescue me. He loved me enough not to let me go, even as far as I went.

He rescued me from my life, from the future Satan had planned for me that I was willingly walking into, and even from how painful this year would've been without Him. It's true that my happily ever after is in Heaven but I don't deserve what He's given me here either. I'm so thankful.

When I first read this Scripture, I said out loud, "Oh my gosh, this is my life on paper."

In context, the Israelites were slaves in Babylon. I'm sure it was hard for them to see God's goodness in their future.

But this passage is a promise from God that if they turned back to Him and sought Him with their whole hearts, He would set them free. He promised that if they grabbed His hand, He would walk them out of the desert. And He promised to purify them as He rebuilt all that had been torn down.

God has amazing plans for us. He wants to set us free from whatever is holding us captive. He will come and find us in the desert, no matter how long we've been walking or how far we are into it. He'll find us to free us.

But there's one condition: that you go with Him.

God's responsibility is to set you free and yours is to walk with Him. Then you'll be able to see the hopeful, prosperous future He already has planned.

You may not be able to see it or even imagine it now. I know I couldn't - and probably still can't for whatever lies ahead. But as you seek Him with your whole heart He'll show it to you.

God will always come find you.

Seek God with all your heart. Grab His hand and let Him lead you out of whatever desert you're in.

GOD WILL COME FIND YOU

GOD,

PLEASE SAVE ME FROM MYSELF.

AMEN

HEBREWS 2:14-18

I haven't had sex or even kissed anyone in over seven years.

I know that statement will shock some people, especially considering what I've shared with you so far in this book. Honestly, I never thought I'd be that girl. And even today, sometimes I look in the mirror like, "Who are you?"

When I think about my relationship with God, one of the things I'm most thankful for is Him setting me free from myself. In trying to figure out who I was, it feels like I did everything possible to ruin my life. I was seriously terrible at keeping myself safe, whole, or loved.

Turns out that God is a way better God than I am. And when I think of what Jesus had to do to save me from myself, I can't believe anyone loved me that much.

Think about this. Jesus left the glory of Heaven. Heaven dude! And stayed on Earth for 33 years. Then He suffered and died voluntarily. Just so He could relate to us in our humanity and set us free from the pain of our own choices. Now that's love!

Jesus was tempted in every way we are and has suffered through every feeling we feel. He understands how challenging this is. Which is why He came. He came to make living this life possible now and worth it in eternity.

Jesus came to set us free from having to get drunk to have fun, or use sex as a bribe for love. He came to set us free from using other people to numb and then feeling more pain when it blows up in our faces. He came to set us free from the self-harming behavior and self-condemning thoughts that we fight through every day.

You can still choose to do all of those things. But Jesus is offering you true freedom and joy in their place.

It's not too good to be true. There's no bad deal here. You can be free from anything that's ever had you in bondge in this life and then go to Heaven.

CHALLENGE:

Read the Gospel of Matthew and look for ways that Jesus can relate to you in your humanity.

DON'T PLAY WITH FIRE

MARK 9:43-48

I almost said, "Wow," out loud.

My friend and I were at an event when I turned around to notice one of the most beautiful people I'd ever seen walk in.

He looked like the type that I knew was dangerous but would've tried anyway just to prove I could get him. So when he approached me I had two options: flirt with the situation and play with fire, or run.

I was definitely tempted. Sometimes I miss the thrill of knowing I could get burnt by something but controlling it enough not to. Still, instead of giving in I kept the conversation light, ended it quickly, and spent the rest of the evening on the other side of the room enjoying the music.

Because when you play with fire there's a fine line between feeling the heat and having it burn your hand. I had crossed that line too many times.

That's how I look at this Scripture. God is telling us not to play with fire, literally and figuratively. He doesn't want us to be walking around without hands, feet and eyes. He's simply telling us to do whatever it takes to keep ourselves from falling into a sin we can't get out of.

Playing with the things that have burnt us in the past isn't wise. Neither is keeping them around. Because none of us are strong enough to control ourselves all the time.

Cut them off quickly and completely.

Then build your life with God into something you love so much that you're not willing to risk burning it down. Because if you're okay sitting in your house and playing with fire in your living room, you don't recognize the value of your house.

Temptations don't go away. The things you gave up for God will be the same things that threaten to pull you away from Him for the rest of your life.

There will always be that moment "your type" walks in, that boundary you want to flirt with, that standard that seems too strict, and that opportunity you know you shouldn't take.

But you'll stay free when you're convinced that the consequences of entertaining sin hurt more than cutting off the temptation.

CHALLENGE:

When you're tempted to flirt with something that once had you in chains, remind yourself of the pain it caused you and others.

I TIMOTHY 1:12-17

Your life is evidence.

I was in a Bible study with one of my friends telling her about my life before God when her face went from engaged listening to disbelief.

"What's wrong?" I said.

She replied, "It's just crazy because knowing you now, I can't even picture you saying a cuss word, let alone doing everything else you're talking about."

I wanted to laugh because people say that to me often and for me, knowing my past, it seems so far fetched. But I knew she was serious.

Instead of laughing I said what I always say. "Amen, God is good." Which is true too.

Part of me wishes I would've started following God earlier in my life, or made fewer mistakes, so I would have fewer wounds to heal from. Then I remember all of the people who think they can't change or those with pasts they're ashamed of and I change my mind.

Every single painful thing I've been through is worth being able to show people that this life with God is real and possible.

These Scriptures specifically highlight God's trust and patience, which I love because I feel like God courted me for years.

He waited for me to choose Him while He was pursuing, rescuing, comforting and loving me at every turn. I walked away, He would take me back. And then once He finally did save me, He started trusting me to do His work.

When I think about it, it never makes sense. If I was God, I would've given up on me a long time before I actually listened. But He was that patient and trusting with me so I could be an example of His patience and trust for everyone.

That's why He sets us free. Our lives are meant to be the evidence of His power to help, heal and change people like us.

So wherever you are on your journey to freedom, know that God has plans for you to impact people. He hasn't given up on you, no matter where you are, what you've done or even what you're doing.

He's patiently waiting to grant you the true freedom that's only found in Him and use you to help others find theirs also.

Seek out someone who has been set free in areas you're struggling with and commit to sharing with others about the ways you've been set free.

SET FREE TO FREE OTHERS

10. HO

PEFUL

(A Conversation About Hope)

MY TRUE HOPE CAME WHEN I
DISCOVERED HOPE EXTENDED FAR PAST
THE BASKETBALL COURT.

Hope - To expect with confidence[8]

I previously shared part of this story with you in chapter seven, Coping With Jesus. But I want to put it in context of the bigger picture.

Memory refresh...

It was my fourth year in the WNBA and I was coming off seven months of rehabbing a potentially career-ending broken kneecap - the most painful thing I'd ever felt. But I worked my butt off and came back in the best shape of my life. I signed with arguably the best team in Turkey to make my return to the court during the WNBA off-season.

Three games in, I was averaging over 20 points and 10 rebounds. It was the breakout season I had hoped four years for.

Until our fourth game. I jumped up to catch a pass, landed, pivoted, and felt like someone had just kicked me right above my heel.

I'd heard so many people describe this same injury and I knew exactly what had happened. I had just torn my Achilles tendon.

With the memories of my last injury and the arduous rehab journey still fresh in my mind, I collapsed to the floor weeping, "I can't do this again, I can't do this again." At the time I really did believe that. My hope was shattered.

Three weeks after I'd had surgery and traveled back to the States came the horrible night you read about with the weed, the gun, and the alcohol.

Thankfully my story didn't end there.

When I woke up the next morning from that devastating night, I reasoned that God had answered my prayer for help by sending sleep and the chance of another day.

I considered it a sign that He had something else for me to do. For the first moment since my injury, I had hope.

When I came back to the WNBA that next season, even though I did have challenges to work through, there were still moments and even games that felt incredible. I belonged out there with the best women players in the world.

For me the game didn't stop being fulfilling just because I wasn't "the same." I still contributed and I still loved it.

But really, my true hope came when I discovered that hope extended far past the basketball court.

When I look back, I'm extremely grateful that I hoped in basketball enough to stay alive that night. And that I was eventually able to come back and play.

It's sad too, though. The thought of losing a temporary game got me to the point where I felt like life wasn't worth living anymore. Whatever our hope is in, we give the power to break us when it proves itself unreliable.

So in actuality, my hope in basketball didn't save me. My hope in basketball is what had me ready to take my own life in the first place when it failed me.

While me getting back on the basketball court was a happy event, the happy ending is ultimately realizing that my hope wasn't in basketball or anything else. The happy ending is placing my hope in God instead.

We can put our confidence in many different things and those things can all be taken away with a phone call, an injury, or a decision, and without a moment's notice.

But putting our hope in God means that we're hoping in the one thing that's constant. It means that life is always worth living because no matter what happens, God can always bring something good out of it.

Even if...

You're playing hurt for a while.
You can't do what you did before.
You're never famous.
You get sick.
You lose a loved one.
All your hope in the world is taken away.

Even if all those things happen, you can still have hope in God.

Hope in the promise that God still has a purpose for you.
Hope in the fact that He has a life of beauty for you to find.
Hope in the unique impact He designed in advance for you to have.
And overall hope in the promise of spending eternity with God.

True hope enables perseverance and a joyful life.

Let's study it out.

DEAR GOD,

THANK YOU IN ADVANCE.

AMEN

A STUDY ON HOPE

Please read each Scripture before you read each devotional.
God's words are more important than mine.

PSALM 27:13-14

God doesn't change with the seasons.

Sixth grade was my first year living with Daddy and Mom in Washington after previously only spending the summers with them. I had to adjust to the constant rain of the Pacific Northwest, make all new friends and deal with bullies at school.

The biggest hurdle, though, was adapting to a life of structure that was completely different from the chaotic freedom I was used to. My parents and I argued often trying to figure it out. It was a long, grueling year.

As the summer neared, I was hoping we'd return to the carefree life of sleep-overs, craft nights and other fun events we had before. But I was also afraid our fights during the year would change things.

One day, a couple of weeks before school let out, Mom and Daddy told my sisters and me to come upstairs because they had a surprise for us. They made us close our eyes and all hold hands as they led us outside. I didn't peek, even though I was desperate to know what it was.

I heard them both say, "One, two, three! Open your eyes!"

When we opened them there was a brand new, giant trampoline sitting right in the middle of our backyard. We screamed, jumped up and down, hugged them, and it felt like we said thank you a hundred times as we jumped onto it and started bouncing.

That was the beginning of the best summer yet! We spent every day outside.

It also showed me that just because living with Mom and Daddy during the year was different, that didn't mean the summers wouldn't still be fun. They loved us year-round and nothing we did changed that.

Hoping in God is very similar.

Life can't be summer vacation all the time. There are going to be tough seasons we go through. We'll have to navigate times of growth and change, and the challenges that come with those. Repeated disappointment can make it harder for us to believe that something good is right around the corner.

However, we can't let the fact that God has to parent during the hard times make us forget that He also loves to spoil us. God is the same. And while life requires different aspects of Him at different times, His love never changes.

No matter what is happening in the present, you can remain confident that you will see the future goodness of God. Continue to look forward in

Let your confidence in the future be based on who God has already shown Himself to be. Don't let challenges make you question it.

FAITH IS BELIEF IN THE PRESENT.

HOPE IS BELIEF IN THE FUTURE.

MATTHEW 7:9-11

God loves "shopping" for you.

I hate Christmas shopping in person. The crowds, the waits, the money. It's all intense. But last year, since I procrastinated on getting Kingston and Missy their gifts, I didn't have time to order anything.

I initially walked into Target with a time limit and a budget. When I saw the selection, the time limit went out the window immediately and I spent an hour walking up and down the aisles looking for the perfect gifts.

Then I saw it. It was a little girl's vanity mirror with mermaids, lights and music that played when you opened it. It was perfect. It was also significantly more than I wanted to spend.

I kept walking around, hoping I would find something more perfect and less expensive, but no luck. That gift felt like it already had Missy's name on it. There went the budget too.

I grabbed it, along with a soccer goal for Kingston, and headed back to the house to get them wrapped.

At six the next morning Kingston and Missy woke up and ran into the living room, anxious to see what they'd gotten.

When they opened the vanity and soccer goal, their smiles, hugs and thank you's were worth every minute and every penny I had spent. Even better was watching them play and enjoy their gifts, knowing they were from me.

If we, as imperfect humans care enough to surprise those we love with things they love, how much more does a perfect Father?

When our gifts take longer than we'd like we can be tempted to picture God sitting up in Heaven, intentionally holding back the things we want. Instead, it's more like God is picking out the perfect gifts, getting them ready, and waiting until the perfect time to give them to us.

Sometimes we get angry at God, thinking He's saying, "no," when really his answer was, "not yet," or, "I have something better."

Trust His heart for you. God loves to go above and beyond. And He loves watching you enjoy the gifts He's given you. So no matter what the gift is, when it gets there or how long you have to wait for it, you can be sure it's going to be amazing.

Hope in every day like it's Christmas morning because God knows how to give good gifts.

Think back to a time when you put great effort into finding someone the perfect gift. Picture God doing that for you and let it inspire you to approach every morning with the excitement of Christmas.

GOD GIVES THE BEST GIFTS

HEBREWS 6:19-20

The night my dream came true, I cried myself to sleep.

I had waited seven years for the moment my name was called. Dreamt about it, talked about it, hoped for it. And when it finally came, it was amazing.

"With the second overall pick in the WNBA Draft, the Sacramento Monarchs select Chantelle Anderson from Vanderbilt University."

All of my hard work, the countless hours of practice, film sessions, bus rides, all of it, were worth it for that moment. I hugged my parents, walked up on stage, took pictures, gave interviews, called my new coach, and went out to dinner afterward. It was a beautiful day.

That night though, as I was laying in my hotel room alone, I had the weirdest feeling.

I had hoped for that moment since the first time I heard of the WNBA. But I thought getting there would change me. I thought everything would make sense and it would delete my questions of self-doubt. I thought I'd finally feel like enough.

I didn't. I was still the same me, just with one more accomplishment checked off on my long list of goals. I fell asleep crying in disappointment.

We were made to live in hope but Jesus is supposed to be the anchor we tie that hope to. Not a destination, an accomplishment, a relationship or a title.

Part of Satan's deception is to sell us the idea that everything we've ever wanted is right around the corner in chasing everything but God. It's not true. But he's really great at marketing like it is. In reality, none of those things will fulfill us.

That doesn't mean we can't want and pursue them. God wants us to practice excellence. It does mean we can't be defined by them.

In your mind, regardless of anything else:

God choosing you has to make you enough.
God saying you're important has to make you enough.
God defending you has to make you enough.
God having a plan for you has to make you enough.
God saving you has to make you enough.

If your worthiness, identity, validation, peace and happiness are dependent on anything other than who God is and how much He loves you, your hope is misplaced. You're trusting in the result instead of the God who controls the result.

Anchor your hope in the promise of living this life and eternity with God through Jesus. If that doesn't make you feel like enough, nothing else will.

Tie your hope to who Jesus is now instead of who your accomplishments, titles and relationships will make you in the future. Chase Him above all else.

GOD MADE YOU ENOUGH
GOD MAKES YOU ENOUGH

EXODUS 14:10-31

God is a God of miracles.

When I was in fourth grade, I wrote a play called Mr. Linden's Library. It was about a little girl who loved to read so much that she got sucked into one of her uncle's magical books for the adventure of a lifetime.

Kristin and I learned our lines, drew a background set on big white paper and used our toys as props. Our sister, Amber, was too young to memorize any lines so she played a rock in one scene and a tree in another.

When we put on our grand performance for Mom and Daddy in the living room, they gave us such a standing ovation you would've thought we deserved an Oscar.

Truthfully, I wrote the story because I used to ask God all the time to get sucked into one of my own fantasy books.

Kids believe anything can happen. Then we grow up, learn the rules of life and stop believing in the miraculous. That is practical in some ways. However, we can't let practicality take away our belief in miracles when we follow a God of miracles.

In this passage, the Israelites were definitely having a "God, what the heck?!" moment. Can you imagine how they felt after going through ten plagues to escape Egypt, only to find themselves about to die in the desert with nowhere to go? I'm sure it felt like a lot of wasted time, energy and hope.

Yet they had quickly forgotten all the miracles that got them to that place. They had forgotten how big their God was or how much He loved them. They had forgotten God's resume and let their fear erase their belief in miracles.

I love that Moses went to God and God was like, "Chill. Why are you even freaking out?" Then He handled the situation in a way no one could have expected it.

When you serve a God of miracles, there is always a reason to hope.

Whenever I'm looking at a circumstance that I'm starting to lose hope in, Kristin says, "It's that way until it's not." Just like the Israelites were pinned against the Red Sea until they weren't.

The key is, you have to believe that God can make something happen even when you don't see how. To hope, you have to believe that God is the God of miracles.

Read about different miracles God performed in the Bible. Ask Him to help you believe He can show up for you in the same way.

GOD WILL ALWAYS SHOW UP WHERE HE TOLD YOU TO BE.

DANIEL 3:16-18

God, even if you don't...

When you're single and trying not to be, a lot of people give you advice. I feel like I've heard it all. One I hated for a long time was, "Sis, you just have to be surrendered."

For someone who never even has a "Plan B" until "Plan A" doesn't work and then it's just another "Plan A," I had no idea what that meant.

Surrendered as in I don't want it anymore? No, you can still want it.

Surrendered as in I don't think it will happen? No, you have to trust God that it will happen.

Surrendered as in God promises I'll get married and so I just have to wait? No, God actually doesn't promise anyone a spouse.

It wasn't making sense. I was supposed to want something, believe that I was going to get it, but be great with not getting it? How was that even possible? It felt like it went against the very foundation of who I was.

Then I read this passage and I was like, "Ooohhhh, I get it now."

In context, King Nebuchadnezzar threatened to kill Shadrach, Meshach and Abednego by throwing them into a furnace because they wouldn't worship his false idol.

Faith plus surrender sounds like their response. In short, they told the King, "We know God can. We believe God will. But even if God doesn't, we're still going to obey Him."

They were faithful in refusing to dishonor God, hopeful that He would save them, and surrendered to however God decided to handle the situation.

God being God means that His promises are always true, but He gets to decide what they look like in our lives. Surrender takes walking away from God off the table as an option when we don't like His decisions. It replaces our expectations of God with faith in Him.

In my case of being single, my surrender statement sounds like, "I believe God can send me a husband, I believe He will, but even if He doesn't, I'm not leaving Him to be with a man who doesn't follow Him."

Surrender means that whatever the path to Heaven looks like for you, even when it's not what you would choose, you're committing to keep walking with God because you trust any future with Him.

And as you walk, continue believing in and looking for His goodness along the way. There's no true hope without surrender.

Make your loyalty to God non-negotiable. Write out a surrender statement for any area you're having a hard time surrendering to God in.

JAMES 4:1-3

Heart check.

"Can I ask you a random question?"

I was riding in the car one day with my immensely talented friend. I respected her perseverance in grinding towards a successful entertainment career. But there was something that had been on my mind for a while.

"Sure," she said.

"If God gave you everything you're praying for in your career, would you use it for Him?"

She paused. And then transparently said, "That's a great question. I honestly don't know the answer." Her reply was the reason I had asked.

In response, I shared this passage with her. Then I said that I believed God wanted to use her and her talent powerfully, but that maybe He didn't want to bless her efforts because it would pull her away from Him.

We can never be certain about what God is doing or why, but this Scripture gives two reasons why He wouldn't give someone what they wanted.

The first is because they don't ask, which shows a lack of faith. If we're not willing to ask God for something we want, our belief in his power, love or another aspect of His character is weak. We need to strengthen our faith so it can support the gift.

The second reason is that they would use it for their own pleasures instead of God's. That shows a lack of love, loyalty and submission on our part.

Sometimes God wants to give us what we're asking for but won't because we're not willing to use it for His purpose. There's no godly impact if we take His gift and run the other way with it.

That'd be like gifting your spouse a romantic vacation package for you to go on together and then him or her taking someone else instead. Like what? I know I'd be fuming.

The fact that God can do miracles and wants to bless us doesn't mean He's down for a one-sided relationship. God's love is unconditional but His promises are always conditional. Some of us are hoping in God doing His part without doing ours.

So before you ask God why He isn't giving you what you're hoping for, ask yourself the same question I asked my friend: If God gave you everything you're hoping and praying for, would you use it for Him? Would it bring you closer to Him instead of pulling you farther away?

If your response isn't a confident, "Yes and yes!" then you have an answer as to why you might not have what you're hoping for.

Work on your heart and see what God does with it. We have a part to play in our choice to hope.

CHALLENGE:

Ask and answer the questions I asked my friend. Learn more about God's purpose for your life and commit anything He gives you to it.

BE AVAILABLE TO GOD

JUDGES 6:11-16, ISAIAH 60:22

God sees more in you than you do.

In the spring of my 8th-grade year, I went to a basketball camp in Oregon City. At the time, their senior team was ranked number one in the country. All their players got college scholarships and the coaches, Brad Smith and Carl Tinsley, were considered geniuses in the sport.

I'd just recently been introduced to the world of high-level girl's basketball and when I walked into the gym that morning, I was amazed. Then I was terrified.

I saw about 200 girls, so many of them tall like me, who looked like they'd been playing basketball for a lot longer than the year I had.

That day I got my butt kicked. Being shy and withdrawn, I didn't like this new kind of loud, physical basketball. I even cried in front of everyone when I couldn't get a drill right.

At the end of the day, Brad Smith walked up and introduced himself. He said he'd been watching me and could tell I was going to be a very special player.

Then he invited me to play on their senior team. Over the summer they'd be traveling around the U.S. to defend their number one ranking in the best tournaments. And he wanted me to come with them.

I was shocked and confused. I sucked! Why did he want me? Did he have the right person? What the heck was he looking at?

Brad said he'd already talked to Daddy and just needed my okay. Then he reiterated that I was special and that basketball was going to change my life.

As long ago as that conversation was, I can still vividly remember the hopeful feeling of it. Over the years I would often repeat Brad's words to remind me of what the future held.

When the angel appeared to Gideon in the winepress, calling him "mighty warrior," I imagine Gideon felt like I did, looking around wondering, "Mighty warrior? Are you sure you have the right person?"

Gideon wasn't prominent, strong or influential. It would be a monumental job to restore Israel at such a low time and he was far from the obvious choice. But God saw something special in him that he didn't see in himself.

God saw strength that hadn't been built yet.

He saw talent that hadn't been developed and a heart eager to be great.

He saw the resourcefulness to get things done and the passion to use it for good.

God saw boldness that hadn't been cultivated.

He saw a spirit that would keep on fighting and the humility to know he couldn't do it alone.

No one else saw those things, not even Gideon. But God did.

We can spend so much time waiting for someone to believe in us, to acknowledge that we're special. We can look at our appearance, our background, our skills - or lack thereof - and think we're destined to be average.

But God has a special call for each of us. He doesn't need us to be great already because the best coaches turn potential into reality. We just have to say yes to joining His team. And when we do, it will change our lives.

Just like Brad saw something special in me, God sees something special in you. God believes in you and He chose you.

Let what God sees and the call He has for you give you hope in what He will do through you. In His time, He will do it swiftly.

CHALLENGE:

Believe God can make anyone exceptional at any time. Let what
He sees in you motivate you to keep pushing towards the future.

GOD SEES THE GREATNESS HE PUT IN YOU

PHILIPPIANS 3:10-14

Hope is an optimist.

Basketball taught me the beauty of getting paid to live my dream. And when I retired at 29, I refused to spend the rest of my life hating whatever job I ended up with. Nothing inside me could believe God wanted me to live a life I wasn't passionate about.

But I had absolutely no idea what I wanted to do. So I started experimenting with different occupations, trying to find the second calling I was meant for.

In the process, I coached college basketball, started different empowerment platforms, commentated WNBA basketball, sold medical devices, became a corporate speaker, and now I'm in the full-time ministry, writing and speaking about Jesus.

Sometimes it feels like I've lived five lives.

Honestly, I think all of them were to get me here, to what I'm doing now. Still, going all-in at each stop was exhausting, hoping it would be my second calling, then starting over when it wasn't. I had to keep telling myself not to stop and settle, and to keep going.

The way I look at it, I'm just trying to freely live the call God put in my heart, every day. That's it.

Paul inspires me a lot in this area, which is why He's my favorite person in the Bible who's not God.

His successes never satisfied him and his struggles never made him quit. He wouldn't settle for a shallow relationship with God or a stagnant one. He didn't stop at fulfilling 75% of his calling.

Paul's hope was in Heaven with Jesus and every step he took on Earth was pressing towards that call with everything he had.

When we have hope, it doesn't let us quit. Hope inspires us to press on towards the future no matter what happened in the past. It allows us a life of purpose and perseverance.

That doesn't mean we deny the feelings of our humanity or ignore our wounds. It means we walk with God through it all, regardless of what that looks like.

There will always be those moments when you're tempted to look around like, "God, what the heck," and maybe even quit on Him because of what you feel.

In those times, remember that hope always tries. It pushes, it strains, it fights, and it tries again. Because hope has confidence that better is coming, and in the God who will make it so.

Try again. No matter what that looks like. Keep fighting for your relationship with God and the call He has for your life.

TRY AGAIN TO UNDERSTAND
TRY AGAIN TO WORK IT OUT
TRY AGAIN TO BELIEVE
TRY AGAIN TO SEE THE GOOD
TRY AGAIN TO FIND YOUR FAMILY
TRY AGAIN TO LIVE YOUR CALLING
TRY AGAIN TO WALK WITH GOD

ALWAYS TRY AGAIN.

MATTHEW 5:14-16

It's bigger than you.

I first started blogging back when I was still playing basketball. I always had something to say and using my voice allowed people to see me as more than an athlete. As I wrote, I found I had a talent for saying things in a way that would get people's attention and help them consider different perspectives.

I pulled no punches. Even now when I go back and read my old posts I can't believe how bold, crass, and unapologetic I was.

Fast forward to when I started following Jesus, I decided right away that I was going to share my journey through posting on social media.

To me, it didn't make sense not to use the biggest platform in history to share the most important message in history. Plus I've always lived out loud so if I was going to be on social media at all, I really didn't have a choice not to talk about Jesus.

It started with sharing about my own faith journey. As I grew, I started making videos, writing Bible studies, mentoring women, and eventually creating a brand called Confidently His. My goal in starting the brand was to help a million women learn the truth about Jesus and change their lives for Him.

It's been amazing to see women, both ones I knew from my life and who found me online, grow in their relationships with God, get baptized, and even begin teaching other women to follow Jesus.

None of it is because I'm awesome. It's only because God has allowed me to stand on a hill and be a light for Him.

Part of the hope that comes from God setting us free is that we get to help other people find their freedom in Him too. Not in a way that judges people or forces it on them, but by being a visible example of what God has done in our lives.

Too often we let our insecurities about not being perfect stop us from telling people about a perfect God. We hide our light under a bowl. But we don't have to have everything figured out to help someone.

God gave us each a special light that the world needs. If you decide to shine and shine on purpose, there is someone you can reach for God that no one else can.

Stop hiding, step onto the stand and share the light. You were created to make an impact by using every part of your experience to show the love and the hope of God. Fill yourself with Jesus' light and then show others how to do the same.

YOU ARE THEIR HOPE FOR HOPE IN JESUS

ROMANS 10:16-17, HEBREWS 11:1

Confession: When I like a guy, I study him.

The last time I had a new crush was fun and also kind of terrifying.

When I started liking him I wanted to be around him all the time, everything he said was either funny or interesting, he made every outfit look good and I loved hearing him talk about his dreams.

But I also wondered if he was who I thought he was. Because that - not all the other stuff - would tell me if hoping for a future together made sense.

So what did I do? Stalk his social media of course. You know we all do it.

I also started watching how he treated people, how hard he worked, and how devoted to God he was. I read his messages a couple of times, at least, before responding. Partly so I didn't say anything stupid, but mostly so I didn't miss anything that would tell me more about who he was. Overall, I started studying him.

The end goal was to learn as much about him as possible, doing everything I could to make sure my hope for a future with him wouldn't leave me disappointed.

It's the same with God. Knowledge of God leads to faith in Him, which allows hope for our future together.

If I could highlight any one practical in this book as the key to getting me through hard times, this is it. As I was fighting hopelessness through the turmoil of this year, I never stopped trying to learn more about God so I could believe Him.

I did have questions. Believing can be challenging at times because the Bible says a lot of things I don't like. Still, I have to trust that the One who created the universe knows more than I do.

The empowering part about believing the Bible is that I get to believe God's promises for my life are true. If the Bible is true, I can confidently hope in what it promises me.

I didn't always have that faith. But I got to a point where nothing else I tried was working and I was desperate to see a change in my life. So I tried the Bible on the slim chance that it would lead me to God and ended up accidentally believing it.

As an intellectual, it was hard because I tend to live in my head instead of my heart. You can't intellectualize faith. You have to build it.

The biggest influence on your ability to hope in the future will be your faith in the God who promises it. The more you get to know Him, the more you'll be able to trust who He is and hope in what He will do.

Need hope? Get faith.

CHALLENGE:

Read God's Word like you read your crush's text messages. P.S. I know it's like a really, really long text, so if you need help I got you. ConfidentlyHis.com.

STUDY GOD, ON PURPOSE.

HOPE IN GOD'S LOVE
HOPE IN GOD'S PATIENCE
HOPE IN GOD'S KINDNESS
HOPE IN GOD'S GOODWILL
HOPE IN GOD'S MODESTY
HOPE IN GOD'S HUMILITY
HOPE IN GOD'S PATIENCE
HOPE IN GOD'S HONOR
HOPE IN GOD'S CONSIDERATION
HOPE IN GOD'S GRACE
HOPE IN GOD'S FORGIVENESS
HOPE IN GOD'S GOODNESS
HOPE IN GOD'S TRUTH
HOPE IN GOD'S PROTECTION
HOPE IN GOD'S TRUST
HOPE IN GOD'S HOPE
HOPE IN GOD'S PERSEVERANCE
HOPE IN GOD'S RELIABILITY

HOPE IN GOD.

OUTRO

Wow, this is the end! We've been through a lot together. We've laughed, cried and reflected through 100 devotionals. We made it!

I can't begin to tell you how transformative this book was for me. Writing it helped me cling to God and His Scriptures during one of the most turbulent times of my life.

I pray that it's been impactful for you too. You were a big part of my motivation and for you to walk with me in the middle of your storm is a privilege I don't take lightly.

My desire is that what we've talked about inspires you to continue in your deeper and forever conversation with God.

I hope that as you go through the ups and downs of life, this is one book you pick up to encourage you. I hope that eventually your favorite devotionals are all marked up, your journal is full of new entries, and your favorite quotes are hung on your wall as reminders. I know mine are.

My ultimate prayer is that you believe how loved and valuable you are to God and fall deeper in love with Him every day. Life with God's love is enough.

I do hope that we'll keep in touch over social media and at future events. Please don't hesitate to reach out for prayer, Bible studies or even to share how God came through for you in your "God, what the heck?!" moments.

I can't wait to see what God has up next. I don't know what it is, but I do know His plans for you are incredible and He'll be there every step of the way. Cheers to the adventure!

In grace and gratitude,

Chantelle

WHAT NOW?

STAY IN TOUCH OF COURSE!

Interact with all *God, What The Heck?!* content on www.GodWhatTheHeck.com

Connect on Instagram! @MissChantelle

Share your reflections, challenges, pictures, and connect with others doing the same by using the hashtag #GodWhatTheHeckBook

Also join the Confidently His community at www.ConfidentlyHis.com

Excited to continue this journey online!

DEFINITIONS

1   "grief." Dictionary.com, s.v. https://www.dictionary.com/browse/grief (19 August 2020)

2   Strong, J., Strong, J. and Strong, J., 1990. The Exhaustive Concordance Of The Bible. 1st ed. Peabody, Mass.: Hendrickson Publishers.

3   "shame." Merriam-Webster.com. 2011. https://www.merriam-webster.com (14 November 2020)

4   "cope." Merriam-Webster.com. 2011. https://www.merriam-webster.com (20 November 2020)

5   "cistern." Merriam-Webster.com. 2011. https://www.merriam-webster.com (20 November 2020)

6   "stronghold." Merriam-Webster.com. 2011. https://www.merriam-webster.com (20 November 2020)

7   "restore." Merriam-Webster.com. 2011. https://www.merriam-webster.com (23 November 2020)

8   "hope." Merriam-Webster.com. 2011. https://www.merriam-webster.com (29 November 2020)

THANK YOU'S

There are too many people to thank individually on this page. If I mentioned you by name in this book, you have played an irreplaceable part in my continuing journey to become the woman God created me to be. And for that, I am and will be eternally grateful.

To Mommy, for loving me the best you could with the circumstances you were given.

To Mom, for your selfless servitude in loving three adopted girls as your own, then and now.

To Kristin, for your wisdom and unwavering belief in everything I do.

To Amber, for always being my little sister but now becoming an amazing friend.

To Lee, for your loyalty and friendship along the path of this crazy discipleship life.

To Coach Foster and Coach Gaudet, for teaching me so much about life and God through basketball.

To my spiritual mentors over the last seven years - Lynn, Elizabeth, Jalisa, Helen, Lauren, Emma, and Jeraldine - for your love, wisdom and sacrifice in helping me grow in maturity for God.

To Christine, for your tiresless and beautiful editing of this book - and the pep talks along the way.

To you, for reading this and playing a part in God's plan for my life.

Most of all - of course - to God. This book and my life are my thank you, and it will still fall far short of all You deserve.

DEAR DADDY,

I just wrote a whole book of words but can never find any when I try to tell you what you mean to me. There are still only tears.

So as I acknowledge this is far more shallow than my feelings go, I'll say thank you. Your fierce love and dedication to being a great Daddy made it easier for me to accept the reality of God's love.

Thank you for falling in love with Mom. You choosing her changed my life.

And thank you for always letting me know you were proud of me, no matter what I was doing. Your constant belief has allowed me to chase my dreams, even up to now.

I find comfort in the fact that anyone who reads this book and gets a little closer to God will do so, in a large part, because of your life. I pray God uses it powerfully, and that it's an addition to your legacy.

I miss you so much. I'll always be a Daddy's girl. And I know this wouldn't hurt so much if we didn't love so much.

Thank you for being the best. I love you always.

"WITH THIS IN MIND, WE CONSTANTLY PRAY FOR YOU, THAT

OUR GOD MAY MAKE YOU WORTHY OF HIS CALLING, AND THAT

BY HIS POWER HE MAY BRING TO FRUITION YOUR EVERY DESIRE

FOR GOODNESS AND YOUR EVERY DEED PROMPTED BY FAITH."

– 2 THESSALONIANS 1:11 NIV

DEAR GOD,

THANK YOU FOR EVERY PERSON READING THIS PAGE. KEEP THIER EYES OPEN AND HEART SOFT TO YOUR TRUTH. I PRAY THEY NEVER STOP PURSUING YOU. PLEASE BLESS THEIR EVERY STEP MOTIVATED BY LOVE, PROTECT THEM FROM ANYTHING OUTSIDE OF YOUR WILL, AND HELP THEM DREAM BIG DREAMS THAT WILL BRING YOU GLORY ON EARTH AND IN HEAVEN. THANK YOU FOR LOVING US MORE THAN WE'LL EVER UNDERSTAND OR DESERVE. HELP US TO LIVE IN JESUS NAME TODAY AND EVERY DAY.

AMEN

Printed in Great Britain
by Amazon

86075463R00163